LIZ LOCHHEAD

Liz Lochhead's books include *Dreaming Frankenstein and Collected Poems*; *Penguin Modern Poets Four*; and the collection of theatre lyrics and performance pieces *True Confessions*. Already a performer of her own work and a frequent broadcaster, she began writing for the theatre in 1980. Among her plays are *Blood and Ice*; *Mary Queen of Scots Got Her Head Chopped Off*; *Quelques Fleurs*; *Cuba*; *Britannia Rules*; *Perfect Days* and translation/adaptations including Stoker's *Dracula*; *The York Mysteries*; Chekhov's *Three Sisters*; Euripides' *Medea* and these sparkling Molière versions. *Perfect Days* and *Medea* are also published by Nick Hern Books, under whose imprint her *Collected Plays* will be published.

Liz was educated at Glasgow School of Art, where she graduated in Drawing and Painting in 1970. She is married and lives in Glasgow's West End.

Other Plays from Scotland

SCOT-FREE
New Scottish Plays
Alasdair Cameron (ed,)

John Byrne
WRITER'S CRAMP

John Clifford
LOSING VENICE

Anne Marie Di Mambro
THE LETTER-BOX

Chris Hannan
ELIZABETH GORDON QUINN

John McKay
DEAD DAD DOG

Rona Munro
SATURDAY AT THE
    COMMODORE

Tony Roper
THE STEAMIE

SCOTLAND PLAYS
New Scottish Drama
Philip Howard (ed.)

Catherine Czerkawska
WORMWOOD

Ann Marie Di Mambro
BROTHERS OF THUNDER

Stephen Greenhorn
PASSING PLACES

David Greig
ONE WAY STREET

Liz Lochhead
QUELQUES FLEURS

Linda McLean
ONE GOOD BEATING

Iain Crichton Smith
LAZYBED

Henry Adam
AMONG UNBROKEN HEARTS

Kate Atkinson
ABANDONMENT

John Clifford
LIGHT IN THE VILLAGE

Mike Cullen
ANNA WEISS

Riccardo Galgani
Linda McLean
Iain Crichton Smith
FAMILY

Sue Glover
SHETLAND SAGA

Stephen Greenhorn
PASSING PLACES

Liz Lochhead
MEDEA (after Euripides)
PERFECT DAYS

Rono Munro
THE MAIDEN STONE
RIDDANCE
YOUR TURN TO CLEAN
    THE STAIR & FUGUE

Stuart Paterson
CINDERELLA
HANSEL AND GRETEL
KING OF THE FIELDS

Michel Tremblay
THE GUID SISTERS

Other Plays from Molière

DON JUAN
(trans. by Kenneth McLeish)

THE HYPOCHONDRIAC
(trans. by Martin Sorrell)

THE LEARNED LADIES
(trans. by A.R.Waller)

TARTUFFE
(trans. by Martin Sorrell)

Liz Lochhead

MISERYGUTS
&
TARTUFFE

two plays by Molière

NICK HERN BOOKS
London
www.nickhernbooks.co.uk

A Nick Hern Book

This edition of *Misery Guts* and *Tartuffe* first published in
Great Britain in 2002 as a paperback original by Nick Hern Books Ltd,
14 Larden Road, London W3 7ST

Misery Guts copyright © 2002 Liz Lochhead
Tartuffe copyright © 1985, 2002 Liz Lochhead

Tartuffe first published in 1985 jointly by Polygon, Edinburgh,
and Third Eye Centre, Glasgow

Liz Lochhead has asserted her right to be identified as
the author of these works

Cover design: Ned Hoste, 2H

Typeset by Country Setting, Kingsdown, Kent CT14 8ES
Printed by Bookmarque, Croydon, Surrey

ISBN 1 85459 680 2

A CIP catalogue record for this book is available from
the British Library

Contents

Introduction

Poor old Monsieur Poquelin, upholsterer by Royal Appointment to Louis XIV. His son, Jean-Baptiste, is a great disappointment. First he shows no interest whatsoever in the family trade. Then, after an expensive education at the University of Orleans, when the boy is finally coming out for a lawyer does he not – what a cliché – fall for an actress. Worse still, beautiful, red-haired and five years his senior, Madeleine Béjart persuades him they'll set up a two-sous theatre company with a handful of rackety relatives from her tribe of troupers. Finally he has to go and change his name to Molière.

Dad didn't know his son was destined to become one of the world's greatest comic playwrights. One whose plays are universal in their application yet untranslatable, according to the conventional wisdom. A snooty contributor to *The Oxford Companion to the Theatre* believes that, 'In transit the wit evaporates and only a skeleton plot is left. This, however, will not deter people from trying.'

Scots playwrights, more than most, have been guilty of this foolhardy exercise, and it is fun to speculate on the reasons for this perennially re-sprouting branch of the Auld Alliance. Is it because we have no plays of our own from this time? Are we filling a gap? Certainly our Reformation, early and thorough, stamped out all drama and dramatic writing for centuries. This means that the indigenous product seems to consist of Lyndsay's 1540 *Ane Satyre of the Thrie Estaitis* – and ane satire is definitely not enough. We have no Scottish Jacobean tragedies, no Scottish Restoration comedies. Our greatest dramatist that never was, Burns, confined himself to the dramatic monologue purely in poetic form, to the multiple lyric voices of his many conflicting personae.

But why Molière? What is there about this particular seventeenth-century Frenchman that has made him our darling? Well, for one thing, he's a lot funnier than Corneille or Racine, and our great Scottish theatre actors have tended to be comedians.

The front of Noel Peacock's book *Molière in Scotland* features a photograph of Duncan MacRae as Tartuffe. He's fingering the décolletage of Elmire with such a ridiculous and naked expression of foolish lust on his skinny long-mouthed, long-nebbed face and in his glittering eye that I long to have seen that production. Robert Kemp's *Let Wives Tak Tent*, a bonny prose translation of *L'École des Femmes*, starred a hideously and hilariously predatory Rikki Fulton as the old man painfully in love with the young girl. Later he and Denise Coffey, under the Stanley Baxter-ish pseudonym *Rabaith*, rendered *Le Bourgeois Gentilhomme* as *A Wee Touch of Class*.

Some of the best recent Molière in Scots is by Hector MacMillan: *The Hypocondriack*, revived last season in a riot of a production at Edinburgh's Royal Lyceum, and his *Le Bourgeois Gentilhomme, Noblesse Oblige.* MacMillan's prose is a vigorous eighteenth-century' Scots – this being for MacMillan a kind of golden age for the language when both aristocrat and commoner spoke the same unashamed Scots tongue. It also served the elegant verse translation MacMillan did for a fine radio production of *Le Misanthrope*. Other Scots versions have also been immensely popular, among them Victor Carin's *The Hypocondriack*, Kemp's *The Laird o Grippy* from *L'Avare*, James Scotland's *The Holy Terror* and *A Surgeon for Lucinda*, and Gordon Croll's *Torduff: a Richt Holy Willie*. How very similar are some of Molière's characters to our own Scottish literary archetypes.

If there is whiff of a certain vigorous vulgarity in the air, a music-hall broadness, surely this is better than the stilted and mannered orthodoxies of the Comédie Française? In their meticulously costumed productions at France's National Theatre in Paris the actors, upholstered and brocaded like something from M. Poquelin's own workshop, wheel themselves about the stage declaiming 'in the seventeenth-century fashion'. As if such a thing could be retrieved, far less preserved in theatrical aspic. We might go a bit light on the philosophy, but at least in Scotland Molière is funny.

If, back then in 1642 in Paris, la belle Madeleine Béjart hadn't so smitten the twenty-year-old Jean Baptiste Poquelin, he'd certainly have made a brilliant lawyer, with his gift for articulating an argument to its baroque conclusion and beyond, but probably he was stuck from the start with the dramatist's imperative – to put both sides of it.

As a wee boy Jean Baptiste had discovered not only did he have an acute talent for mimicking his mother's priest but also what a most satisfactory hullabaloo this caused, with his father in stitches and his devout mother deliciously torn between hilarity and disapproval. Probably it was all laid out in front of him then: his harlequin-chequered life of ironies, of ups and downs, successes and failures, of Paris and the provinces, of plaudits and penury, of patronage lavished and patronage withdrawn, of works written, rewritten, works alternately feted and banned, of forbidden love, of scandals and cuckoldings, of accusations of blasphemy and incest, of utter anguish for himself turned into absolute hilarity for others. The comic drama of his life climaxed in his ludicrous death after being taken ill on stage playing, while they laughed and laughed, the lead role in *The Hypochondriac*. They buried him in unconsecrated ground as befitted a disreputable member of a degenerate profession.

In middle-age Molière married the beautiful Armande Béjart. She was young enough to be his daughter; indeed some said she was exactly that. She was almost certainly Madeleine's, and not her younger sister, as they tried to put about. Do we imagine the old husband with the young wife didn't know what was bound to happen, or that he didn't suffer agonies when it did? That he was able to so vividly dramatise the excruciating sexual jealousies of old Arnolphe in *The School for Wives* and of the cuckolded Alceste, the Misanthrope – and did so while enduring his own – surely makes him doubly cursed? He was suffering bitterly but was cursed to find it bitterly funny. In the plays, these losers are not laughing. They are hilarious because they are tragic. Conversely the pain and darkness only work on us when the productions of the plays are, on the surface of it, just terribly, terribly funny.

Molière and his company were initially influenced by the Italian Players. The great Scaramouche is said to have taught him all he knew, and something of the folk art of the *commedia dell'arte* and its stock comic masks are apparent underneath his unique eccentrics. Every one of his characters is at once a perfect type and also a unique and absolutely live-and-kicking human being suffused with that particular individual's peculiar mania. Each is a slave to some obsession which is destined only to bring about the thing each most deeply fears. A lack of any sense of proportion mars the psyche of all of these characters, but there's a complexity and mystery at the heart of each compulsion. *Why* does Orgon need to believe in the con man Tartuffe? *Why* would a slave to the truth, a compulsive anti-liar like Alceste, fall in love with Célimène and her cheating ways? We do not know why these things are so, but recognise Life is Just Like That.

Because Molière is so wise, certain cloth-eared critics have imagined that the moderates, the 'honnête hommes' – there's always one – represent his own views and bear the burden of 'the moral' of the plays. What is this, *The Waltons*? The plays are too bleakly brilliant for that. Cléante, Mr. Sensible in *Tartuffe*, does nothing but pontificate, endlessly and uselessly stating the rhyming blooming obvious. The worldly and witty realist Philinte in *The Misanthrope* is ironised as morally weaker, somehow less admirable than the monomaniacal Mizz. All the comic energy, and therefore the sympathy, is always with the crazy protagonist. The sensible line never does prevail. When, via a 'deus ex machina' – a happy ending, out of nowhere – we get a sudden reversal to the ideal order of things, it is always ironically implausible.

There are usually trickster con-man figures. Not 'comic characters' because they're highly conscious of exactly what they're doing, but a wickedly witty delight to watch as they so suavely go about their swindling business. Yet when Tartuffe is scuppered by his all too real lust for Elmire we see the deluder deluded. Self-deluded, he becomes deeply, crazily comic too. And then there's the cheeky maid who has a lot more sense

than her master and is not shy of telling him so. Very satisfying
to all of us who love to see authority bucked. All Molière's
female characters are brilliantly realised, wordly wife,
sophisticated cocotte, ingénue, free spirit, prude. The verbal
cat-fight in *The Misanthrope* which ensues between the prudish
Arsinoé and Célimène when the former – for her own good –
'reluctantly' tells the latter what the world is saying about her,
must be one of the best gifts any playwright ever gave a pair of
actresses.

In 1985 I began a version of Molière's *Tartuffe* for Edinburgh's
Royal Lyceum Theatre Company. All I set out to do was a
version for one production for one particular company: that it
has had a longer life is an unexpected bonus. I thought it'd be
in English for Scottish actors to perform in their own accents.
The Scots it emerged in was a big surprise to me. Well, I'd set
it at the end of the First World War, when small businessman
Orgon could've made a lot of money and married a beautiful
young widow; could still plausibly think he could tell his
daughter who to marry; could still be head of a household with
a maid. This was exactly my grandmother's time and her guid
Scots tongue was evidently inside me waiting to be tapped.
Words I didn't know I knew just tumbled out as I got on with
the enormously good fun of my first attempt at a whole play in
rhyming couplets.

When Molière rhymes – many but not all of his plays do, in
Alexandrine couplets – I think the translation ought to as well.
The rhyme is then potentially its own lovely running gag.
Miseryguts, my brand new version of *The Misanthrope*, is very
different from *Tartuffe* in just about every particular except
this. It was written, like many of the earlier Scots Molières,
with a particular actor in mind – Jimmy Chisholm, a comic
genius. Roll over MacRae and Fulton.

Le Misanthrope is Molière's darkest, strangest, therefore
potentially most hilarious anti-comedy. What could be less
funny than to find yourself deeply and hopelessly in love with
someone of whom you know you deeply and fundamentally
disapprove? ('True love is not being blinded by brilliant sex /
into looking at the one you love through rosy tinted specs')
Nothing in this that couldn't be set in the here-and-now. So

(unlike *Tartuffe*) the characters got new names as well as flats in the New Town and Leith. Do they speak Scots? Well, they speak the way these particular Scotsmen and women do right now. Some Scots, yes, some Americanisms, lots of clichés and buzz-words, much casual profanity, I'm afraid. Like life.

LIZ LOCHHEAD

MISERYGUTS

a new translation / adaptation
of Molière's *Le Misanthrope*

for
Tom Logan
and
Tony Cownie

Miseryguts was first presented on 22 March 2002 at the Royal Lyceum Theatre, Edinburgh. Press night was 23 March 2002. The cast was as follows:

ALEX FREW	Jimmy Chisholm
PHIL INNES	Greg Powrie
OSCAR SCOUGALL	John Kielty
CELIA MANN	Cora Bissett
ARCHIE FAIRBAIRN MSP	Ronnie Simon
CLINT ANDREWS MSP	Barrie Hunter
ELLIE BIRD	Helen Lomax
ZOE ARNOTT	Janette Foggo

Director   Tony Cownie

Designer   Geoff Rose

Lightning Designer   Jeanine Davies

Characters

ALEX FREW

PHIL INNES

OSCAR SCOUGALL

CELIA MANN

ARCHIE FAIRBAIRN MSP

CLINT ANDREWS MSP

ELLIE BIRD

ZOE ARNOTT

ACT ONE

A dark office cum sideroom off a gallery in which there is a noisy and rather drunken opening in progress.

Entering, PHIL *in hot pursuit of a moody* ALEX.

PHIL.
  What are you in a state about?

ALEX.
                    Gie's peace!

PHIL.
  Why the mood and when's it gonny cease?

ALEX.
  Beat it, Phil. Best to just fuck off at this stage!

PHIL.
  Listen to me, man, before you fly into a rage!

ALEX.
  I'll fly where I – I don't want to listen!

PHIL.
  Fuck's sake, man! Is there something I'm missin?
  Alex, I'm your pal, but don't you push it –

ALEX.
  That's all very well and good, but maybe I don't wish it,
  your friendship, quite frankly, after what I've seen,
  keep it, mate! I don't know where it's been!
  Your so-called friendship's nothing but a whore
  I don't wish to consort with any more.

PHIL.
  I'm pleasant to people so I've to hang my head in shame?

ALEX.

> You were all over that bastard but couldny mind his name
> when I asked you after: 'who's the long-lost buddy, Phil?'
> Christ! You're such a suck-up sycophant you make me ill!
> He butters them up to their faces, behind their backs decries
> > them!
> Admit it, all of them, you not-so-secretly despise them!
> *Pleasant?* You *worked that room* in fucking order
> of highest down to lowest. In perfect pecking order!
> Tonight at that opening, man, I saw you lick
> enough arse to make a rentboy sick!
> I wouldn't lower myself to act like that! No fear!
> No way Jose, I couldn't *be* that insincere
> Trowel on the flattery? Over my deid boady!
> I'd hang myself before I'd be a toady.

PHIL.

> Alex – and I mean this most sincerely –
> it's scarcely a hanging matter, surely?

ALEX.

> Very funny! It's all a joke to you!

PHIL.

> No, seriously! What would you have me do?

ALEX.

> Be an honest man. Be straight. Get real!
> Talk from the heart! Say what you think and feel.

PHIL.

> Someone swans up to you – all hail fellow, well met!
> You know the face, but who it is you totally forget.
> Are you supposed to tell the truth and shame the devil?
> Hug him back, man, it costs nothing to be civil!
> Ach, it's happened to all of us once or twice
> but so what? Only nice to be nice . . .

ALEX.

> The inherent dishonesty gives me the boke!
> I'm sorry, call me old-fashioned, mibbe that's how folk
> go on these days. It is! Air-kissing, schmoozing people,

smarming them, charming them, basically using people
to make themselves look good in others' eyes.
Cultivating power and influence, and what that buys!
Bullshit rules, they heap compliments most florid
and OTT on everyone, everywhere – it's horrid! –
whether the man's a gem, one of those straight-up guys
or whether he's an utter arse they totally despise!
Look, I'm sorry, it gives friendship a bad name
when you treat any old eejit exactly the same
as the friend you admire beyond admiration
– or so you said! It's a complete devaluation
of the currency if you chuck it about so freely.
How can I be sure that you rate me really?
I can't! I want you to discriminate
between who you care about and who you hate!
Do you think I wish to watch you gush
All over someone you say privately is pish?

PHIL.

You're television's Mr. I-Speak-My-Mind.
That's showbizz. I'm a backroom boy, I find
in the real world – oh, I don't think twice, it is
only polite to conform to social niceties.

ALEX.

Philip, we have to fight against this sham!
It's shit, this nicey-nicey stuff. How sick I am
of phonies, hypocrites, hollow-men
all! Brown-tongues, bullshitters, shallow men
afraid to speak the truth. Plain-dealing's
too scary because we'll hurt someone's feelings!

PHIL.

In social situations, excessive honesty's not right!
It isn't kind. It isn't politic or polite.
Was it perhaps unnecessarily frank
to call that painter's work 'a load of wank.'?
And to his face too! The man was devastated!
Your precious integrity though was unabated
unabashed, uncompromised, immaculate. You
. . . don't seem to mind much if people hate you?

ALEX.
Nope!

PHIL.
You told old Darlinda Duke she trowels
on the slap as thickly as the antique RP vowels
and that she's well past her sell-by date as a presenter?

ALEX.
Yup!

PHIL.
Yon new Holyrood correspondent, you're his prime
tormentor!
Sure, the boy made an arse of it at first, eh?
But did you have to call him the *Anti-Kirsty*?

ALEX.
Absolutely!

PHIL.
You're kidding!

ALEX.
Not one toty bit!
I don't kid on. I say what I think. That's it!
On air. Live interviews. That's when I'm really cooking!
Yeah, take that programme I did looking
at the cinematic oeuvre of Jim Kilsyth. I goes: hey Jimsy
see your films, they are a pile of Celtic whimsy!
But it's not just at *Scotia,* take tonight
at that gallery, why not, I just put folk right
in passing. Thingwy was there, yon actress wifey
wi the big mooth and political ambitions. (Get a life, eh?)
Yon Celine Zed Broon, the woman is a pain.
I says: Haw, Mrs. Glasgow, you can sing nane!
SNP MSP, my arse! Nobody'd vote for you!
The labour supporter's gonny turn their coat for you
because they've seen you on the telly? Aye!
Dream on, baby, pigs'll fly.
Big Duggie McBoggle was stood there in his cowboy boots
effing and cee-ing at one of *Scotia's* suits

who 'Golly Gosh this is raw!' was chuffed to the gutties
I goes: McBoggle might drink like a real writer but he's
no put biro to jotter since yon TV play
that was groundbreaking, aye, but it wisny yesterday!
As for the paintings, I told yon Macaroni fella
his abstracts were watered-down second-hand Frank Stella.
I said Scottish Avant-garde? The notion's bollocks!
The daubs and dribbles on these walls are a load of Pollocks.
Thingwy laughed, yon 'neo-narrative' Glasgow Boy
I said: laugh all you want, I don't specially enjoy
your portraits of sentimentalised violent machismo either!
Slim Bullman's new book won't set the heather
particularly on fire and, yes, I told him so.
Pure lit-crit, but all he wanted was a square go!
Kelvin Cardiff glowered at me – the guy was on drugs
I said: apart from your first book, folk that read you are mugs!
I told yon young black polo-necker Willy Waddle
his *theatre of boring ideas* was absolute twaddle!
He was drinking Chardonnay with yon Arts Council chappy
who smiled at me. I said: you look happy!
Christ knows why, but, since
The state of the Arts in this country is absolute mince.
Oh – the bitch was absolutely beeling, but fuck it, I'll live –
I told Roz Riverbed her plays are rubbish, derivative!
I goes can you no dae nuthin original? The nation's
up to here with your numpty doggerel 'translations'?
She was there with a tribe of haun-knitted lost-the-plots
who wanted me to sign their petition lobbying for Scots
– Scots *the language* – to be taught in schools.
New devolved Scotland? It's a ship of fools!
I said I'm signing nothing, she says *But Alec!*
I says next you'll be asking me to support the Gaelic?
Gaelic! No cunt speaks it! It's moribund!
So *'Oh let's shall we set up a special fund!'*
See, I'm the only person that's no too polite
to tell new devolved Scotland it's a bag of shite.

PHIL.

That's us all tellt! At long last
we get the benefit of Alex Frew, iconoclast!

ALEX.

It depresses me. It does. Because *I care*
– unlike the next man. I do. I despair.

PHIL.

You're melodramatically morose! It is intolerable!
Haw! That thing at the Lyceum! You're as miserable
as yon Alceste character, that gloomy wee dope
in yon Molière play, Alex! The Misanthrope!

ALEX.

Please! Thon was as unrealistic as it was passe!

PHIL.

Don't be such a miseryguts! Away!
I heard you laughing, once. But in real life
your rants'll change neither the world, nor its wife!
I think it's you who's being unrealistic, man.
They're laughing at you! You're the frankness fan
so I'll not say it behind your back: Al, folk
think your honesty campaign's a bit of a joke.

ALEX.

Fine by me! So I'm a joke! That's magic!
If I was 'in step with society' it'd be tragic.
The people around me so totally disgust me
I'm happy that they despise me, trust me!

PHIL.

You'd condemn the whole of humanity?

ALEX.

I loathe human beings and all society.

PHIL.

A somewhat sweeping statement. Eh?
It's staggering! Even in our imperfect world today
surely there are plenty who don't conform –

ALEX.

Everyone I see around me's lower than a worm.
Some are just plain vile and evil, others condone
evil and viciousness by leaving evil-doers alone
to just get on with it with impunity.

Take Candy Tate, that bitch takes every opportunity
to do others down, claw herself another rung up the ladder
and not care who she steps on on the way. She is madder
for success and her own show than anyone in the station
– which is saying something! No one's seen the like of such
                                                    ambition,
blind, blonde and rampant! Behind the girly mask
– which fools nobody except the boss – don't ask!
Of course she did, and she will again!
Sleeping your way to the top? That's the *point* of men
for Candy Tate, hard-as-nails supervixen.
Nobody can stand her! The eyelashes, the tricks'n'
the treacheries are legendary and legion, office politics that
make Machia-fucking-velli look a pussycat.
She wants my slot. Her point is: I'm a writer
so I'm bound to be biased, which is quite a
good argument for a professional presenter like herself?
– Who wouldn't lift a book down from the shelf
except for research purposes for the programme's sake.
Scary! The young Scotsman or (worse) Scots*woman* on
                                                    the make . . .
I despair. Sometimes I think I'll quit the society of men
and go and live up North or somewhere in a but-and-ben.

PHIL.

Oh so nobody likes you, you like nobody
you're away into the garden to eat worms? Can somebody
mibbe explain to me how this particular poet
is going to earn his crust, well? No, he's going to throw it
all away, his glittering career as a top broadcaster
that *I've* worked hard for, and you're a hard task-master,
Alex, face it, you're a maverick – and a bugger to produce!
But worth it! Till this new phase. What's the use
of being so bloody jaundiced and flying into a rage
about how short we fall of the standards of some Golden Age
that is a myth anyway? I just don't get it!
Accept things as they are, Alex! Don't you let it
bug you, because all it is is human nature, so go easy!
– On yourself as well man, because it'll drive you crazy
to rail against everything that's wrong and try and change it!
You'll burst a blood vessel unless you can arrange it

to take folk as they come, just smile, shrug, say 'typical!'
– that's what I do. I decided to get philosophical
and now I just let it all go by me, that's how come
my knickers are as *un*twisted as yours are up your bum!

ALEX.

Well, comrade, old sport, this placability
of yours – can nothing dent your perfect equanimity?
If, God forbid, a friend should utterly betray you,
cheat you out of house and home, do you say you
– if slandered in so disgraceful and dramatic
a way as to *destroy* you – would still stay so phlegmatic?

PHIL.

You rail against design-faults we can't escape!
The selfish-gene's inbuilt. We are the naked ape!
So if the will to survive makes us go the whole hog
to do the other man down, well, it's dog eat dog!
No more surprising than that the vulture
goes for carrion! I repeat. It's human nature.

ALEX.

So I'm to be pounced upon, libeled, torn to bits,
thrown to the lions – Enough! Oh, it's
obvious there's no point talking, so I'll zip it!

PHIL.

I wish you would. I'd like to nip it
in the bud, you know, this . . . nagging worry
that if you don't see off Candy Tate, then you'll be sorry.

ALEX.

I wouldn't lower myself to be concerned.

PHIL.

I've seen others underestimate her and get badly burned.

ALEX.

I'm doing nothing but just wait and see.

PHIL.

I'll pitch *our* projects, but it isn't up to me – !

ALEX.

I know that! Her or me? Who's the better broadcaster!

PHIL.
>You. Obviously. But I've seen that broad master
>quite a repertoire of dirty tricks . . .

ALEX.
>   I'll put an end to it
>without exerting myself unduly.

PHIL.
>   Don't depend on it!

ALEX.
>I'm doing nothing.

PHIL.
>   She's got the patter!
>she talks a good game and she'll –

ALEX.
>   Doesn't matter!

PHIL.
>Don't kid yourself!

ALEX.
>   I'll see what comes to pass.
>If the controller gives in to her he's a bigger ass
>than I think he is, even. Will he back me
>or be professionally suicidal enough to sack me?
>Because if he did, in some ways I'd be quite
>pleased to have the satisfaction of being right.

PHIL.
>You'd be right about the world should that bitch rob
>you of your slot on the Network and take your job?

ALEX.
>Yeah, it'd show how morally bankrupt and perverse
>was every human institution in the universe.

PHIL.
>You are quite ludicrously misanthropic.

ALEX.
>Misanthropic, *moi*?

PHIL.
>   Yup, and on this topic,
>   I just don't get it. There's this moral rectitude
>   you demand of others with such exactitude,
>   this 'absolute integrity' you shove
>   down all our throats, but as for your lady-love –
>   excuse me, is it even in her nature?
>   You're at war with the whole human race except one creature
>   who embodies everything you say you most abhor.
>   You chose pretty perversely a woman to adore!
>   The stepsister Ellie is obviously dead keen.
>   So's that telly critic dame – to be so gratuitously mean
>   to you constantly in print proves the woman is obsessed!
>   But Alex has to pick out Celia Mann from all the rest!
>   You're hooked by Madame High-Maintenance,
>   a manipulative flirt with an eye for the main chance.
>   Ironic that what you find unlivable
>   with in others, in Celia's not just forgivable
>   but adorable, even! Are you blind, man?
>   You know what like she is! Or don't you mind man?

ALEX.
>   Blind? I know what Celia's like, of course.
>   She's been through a crazy time since her divorce
>   – in ways of which I do not necessarily approve –
>   but oh, I love her! Passion does not remove
>   my judgment – and my Celia knows I judge!
>   She loves me for it. The fact that I won't budge
>   in my campaign to make her quit her wicked ways
>   is what she finds so sweet 'bout me she says!

He goes to the door and calls on her from among the crowd.

ALEX.
>   Hey! Celia! Celia, baby, come here my pet! –
>   Phil, I'll make an honest woman of her yet!

PHIL.
>   If you managed that, you could do worse!
>   Are you sure she loves you, man?

ALEX.

    Of course!

    Would I love her if I didn't know she loved me?

PHIL.

    You wouldn't be the first that I can see!

    But if you're so sure that she loves you, then –

ALEX.

    Why am I so exercised about other men?

    She's changed. So've I! We've both had a bellyfull

    of quick affairs! We want a deep-and-meaningful.

PHIL.

    If I was you I'd go for that wee stoater Ellie Bird

    She fancies you rotten, or so I've heard!

    The real you! She sees through all the hype.

    She's smart. She's true! She's just your type.

ALEX.

    You're right. My head tells me every day

    But I'm in love! My heart won't play!

PHIL.

    But Alex, is this Celia the one for you?

    Young OSCAR *sweeps in to the surprise of both men – and*
    the palpable disappointment of ALEX.

OSCAR.

    Alex, you and I don't know each other well, it's true!

    I wish I did though! Celia and I have just been shopping.

    She said let's Do Art, don't sit in channel-hopping,

    c'mon bring Alex your poems, don't think twice,

    he's the most generous of critics, he'll dish out literary advice

    that'll be to die for! I said: but Alex Frew's so famous!

    He's our premiere Scottish poet, he's a friend of Seamus!

    As well as all the telly stuff, *essays*, as a cultural

                                       commentator

    this guy beats the lot! I said: Celia, no honour greater

    than some day to be counted as a friend of such a polymath!

    She said: he'd adore to read your poems, set you on the path

    to publication maybe? Am I talking to myself? Hello!

ALEX.
You talking to me?

OSCAR.
Oh sorry I should go!

ALEX.
No, no! It's just a wee bit of a surprise –
You paint a picture of someone I don't recognise!

OSCAR.
You're Scotland's most high-profile nationalist.
You're in the 'ten most influential' list.

ALEX.
Oscar –

OSCAR.
You won the 'What Scot I'd Actually Like to Shag?'
poll in the *Herald*. The thinking woman's Melvin Bragg!

ALEX.
Oscar –

OSCAR.
– that's what they called you! Go on admit!
As far as I am concerned Alex you're It!

ALEX.
Oscar –

OSCAR.
I'm not kidding, by the way!
You're my hero, and that's not a thing I'd say
to any another man but you in all this land!
I'd be over the moon if you'd just take my hand
and say you'll be my friend and mentor?

ALEX.
Oscar –

OSCAR.
What? Do you consent, or – ?

ALEX.
– Your request, dear Oscar, is awfully flattering
but friendship's surely a more organic thing?

To talk it into being's to deride
the very concept of the thing itself. We can't *decide*!
Will we be friends? Time alone will tell. Who knows!
An unfolding mutual sympathy's the soil in which it grows.

OSCAR.
You're right! Sorry I sort of lost the plot
and jumped the gun. It'll happen. Or not!
Oh, you see how much I need you
and the fruits of your experience – I'll always heed you
and your advice to me. Many thanks, good friend!
You'll set me straight, Alex, on that I can depend!
'It's alright for you, Oscar' – that's what people say.
But me? I'm determined to make my own way
whoever my father is! I don't need to use that!
Nepotism might be one way but I don't choose that.
No, thank you very much! If you've got the talent, I maintain,
you'll succeed on your own terms – no pain, no gain!
So crit my new poem, eh? Be tough, don't fake it!
I'm my father's son so I can take it!

ALEX.
Read it and criticise? That's not what I do!

OSCAR.
Excuse me?

ALEX.
Well, except *professionally*, that's true!
I see you've brought it, and you're most persuasive,
but no, you'd find my honesty far too abrasive.

OSCAR.
Honesty's exactly what I want! I didn't come
so you'd fob me off with 'Very nice dear,' like my Mum.

ALEX.
Well, you've twisted my arm – so bend my ear!

OSCAR.
I don't know if I'll get away with something this explicit here!

ALEX.
Well, Phil – I should have introduced you, sorry that
was rude!

Philip Innes, my producer. Phil here's no prude!

OSCAR.

God! Not in here! Linguistically you're an iconoclast!
I meant in Scotland. But maybe things have changed at last?

ALEX (*aside*).

Do you believe this guy? He's a killer!
as if we'd not had D.H. Lawrence, Henry Miller,
Burroughs – d'you know I've a hunch
this bugger's no even read *The Naked Lunch*!
Oscar, modern Scottish Literature would be much duller
were it not for . . . *Trainspotting* and *Morven Callar*!

OSCAR.

Right . . .

ALEX.

He's never read it. I don't believe it! *Shoot*!

OSCAR.

It's still very much a work in progress, nothing absolute –

ALEX.

– Absolutely! Why don't you fire it at us and we'll see?

OSCAR.

I thought: could I explore my sexuality?
In terms of *language* I mean. It's a bit experimental –

ALEX.

It always is! *Go!*

OSCAR.

I can't stand that sort of sentimental
shite you get in all the literary little mags.
Te-tum-te-tum rhythms! Rhymes! That stuff drags.
I wrote this in a single sitting not to disturb the stream of
consciousness.

ALEX.

Let us be listening to it, nevertheless . . .

OSCAR.

Coming up with the title, that's the bit I hate.

I thought *Cunnilingus*? – A bit Latinate?
Could've plumped for *Oral Sex*. OK, I suppose.
Bit blunt though – a wee bit . . . on the nose?

ALEX.

Spit it out, man! What's in a name?

OSCAR.

I hummed and hawed and puzzled. Then it just came.
This won't appeal to those hung up on bourgeois morality
but here's my Sonnet: *Ode To Orality*.

He begins to declaim. Their faces are a picture.

OSCAR.

O! Violet vulva, my cunilingual quine
Ambrosial fount 'neath Venus' mound
La-la-lovely lubricious nectars I crave!

PHIL.

Interesting. Of the tradition, yet with a post-modern twist.

ALEX.

Violet vulva? Is he a poet or a gynaecologist?

OSCAR.

Orgasmic odours obtrude towards oblivion
O! I swoon too!
Suck! Suck! Suck! Suck! Suck!
Lap! Lap! (*Cat got the cream? Eh pussy? O galore!*)
Ga-loryhole of goodness!

PHIL.

That's good that! Galore! Galory! Get it?
Alex! Galore! Ga-loryhole! As in . . . Oh forget it!

OSCAR.

Lap! Lap! Lap!
La-pretty pudenda, fash'nably bikini-waxed!
Mistress mine, expose
Thy orotund and oozing orifice
And let me kneel before your nether lips and kiss.

PHIL.

Amazing! That really was! Oh wow!

ALEX.
Phil Innes, you bloody hypocrite! What now?

OSCAR.
Philip, I'm flattered! You liked it! Did you really?

PHIL.
Loved it! Like to read it again – on the page ideally!

ALEX.
In another life!

OSCAR.
                    I think you're only being nice!

PHIL.
No!

ALEX.
          Don't encourage him or else we'll have to listen twice!

OSCAR.
Now Alex? Tough criticism! It's money in the bank!
I need your honesty. Be absolutely frank.

ALEX.
These things are always delicate, it . . .

OSCAR.
Tell me the truth. Did you really hate it?
See, what I was trying to –

ALEX.
                              Yeah, yeah, I got it!

OSCAR.
What I'm really asking, Alex – have I caught it?

ALEX.
You've certainly caught something my dear.
Your . . . enthusiasm for your subject comes over loud
                                        and clear.
I was thinking – not apropos this particularly –
but there's a lot of writing about sex these days and generally
one-handed literature comes across . . . ham-fisted.
Perhaps the urge to add to it should occasionally be resisted?

OSCAR.

Are you saying I haven't managed to bring it off?

ALEX.

I didn't say that! But: The Erotic! When it comes to this stuff,
the ecstasy's so ephemeral one can never get it right.
It – as Larkin said of happiness – 'writes white'.

OSCAR.

So I should tear this up and never attempt –

ALEX.

Always! Oscar, these are general points. I'm not exempt!
I've tried, and failed at times, to write what's just impossible!
And – Speaking as A Writer – I hope I always will.

OSCAR.

My poem, then. Have I a voice? It isn't ink
I write in, man, it's blood! But did it make you think?

ALEX.

It did. I thought . . . it was amazing too!

OSCAR.

I know! But how, specifically, did my poem speak to you
and how did you feel as you heard it? Eh Alex? Pray tell!

ALEX.

You really mean it? What went through my head? Oh well:
God save us from the kind of mealy-mouthed bender
who cannot call a cunt a cunt but has to say 'pudenda'.
You call this a *sonnet*, Oscar? Fine!
One, three, seven, *thirteen* – where's the fourteenth line?
Some sonnet! It does not rhyme. Except sporadic'lly,
by accident. The metre lurches spastically.
'Orgasmic odours *obtrude* towards oblivion' ?
See when you wrote this, Oscar? What were you on?
The alliteration's overdone, admit it. A half-assed consonance
that kinda comes and goes . . . No assonance! No resonance!
Your syntax is banjaxed by the way! The only thing that's
                                                                    clear
is that when it comes to poetry you've got Van Gogh's ear.
Nothing written now or in the future that tries to handle
Love or Loving will ever hold a candle

to the sweet and simple lyric from times gone –
Preferably something by Anon!

'Oh Westron wind when wilt thou blow?
The small rain down doth rain.
Christ, that my love were in my arms
And I in my bed again.'

The sheer longing in that song means it will always live
(Even if it were not *the* example of Objective Correlative!)
Oscar, there's only one question for a work of Art:
Is it dead or alive? And has it heart?

'Yestreen when to the trembling string
The dance gaed through the lighted ha
To thee my fancy took its wing
I sat, but neither heard, nor saw:
Though this was fair and that were braw
And yon the toast o a the toun
I sighed, and said amang them a'
'Ye are na Mary Morison'.'

Burns knew how to write love and how to make it
sing out true and sore, there is nothing fake, it
is the real thing. All this postmodern stuff's pretentious pish.

OSCAR.
I think my poem's good!

ALEX.
                              You wish!
Think it's great? Of course you do!
If the author don't think a work 'a work of genius' who?

OSCAR.
You were the one who called the major part of Burns's
                                        oeuvre 'dreich'
'Time Scotland crawled out from under this pile of kailyard
                                        keich!
This is Two Thousand and Two!' That was you! I quote!
On last week's programme! Plus every thing I ever wrote
has given other people pleasure, and that's enough for me!

ALEX.
They're only saying that, as surely even you can see!

OSCAR.

You credit yourself uniquely with an astronomical IQ.

ALEX.

You'd only grant me any intelligence if I praised you.

OSCAR.

My verse will live without the Alex Frew seal of approval.

ALEX.

It'll have to – because it'll never get it, even if you grovel.

OSCAR.

Think you can write? A challenge, *Monsieur Belle-Lettres*.
Same subject, any metre, any style, and you do better!

ALEX.

On the same subject? Guarantee to contemplate the fanny
and come up with better verse than yours? I canny!
Take a cunning linguist to give tongue to such a thing,
                                        I've never tried it
but at least if I made an arse of it like you I'd hide it!

OSCAR.

You arrogant little prick! Don't take that tone – !

ALEX.

I'll take whatever tone I like, you big balloon!

PHIL.

Hey! Guys! Chill! Relax! Time for our beds.

OSCAR.

Negativity rules! Anything creative gets ripped to shreds,
that's Scotland for you! Well, I am out of here!

ALEX.

You sought my frank opinion, mind! I didn't volunteer!

OSCAR *exits in high dudgeon.* PHIL *shakes his head.*

PHIL.

Not funny. Oh my God! Alex, did you have to?
To demolish the poor sap while looking as though you love to!
I could tell he didn't actually want lit-crit!

ALEX.
Don't talk to me!

PHIL.

But –

ALEX.

Leave us for a bit!

PHIL.
Alex, Alex, Alex!

ALEX.

Shutit!

PHIL.

But –

ALEX.

Enough!
I hate insincerity and flattery and lies and stuff!
Why should I do it? Tell me one good reason. One!

PHIL.
Alex, Oscar is the Head of Culture, Art and Entertainment's

son.

End of Act One.

ACT TWO

CELIA*'s trendy, well-designed, modishly untidy open-plan loft.*

ALEX *and* CELIA *are lying in bed, laid back, post coital, smoking cigarettes.*

ALEX.
    Celia, sorry to go on, but I have to make you sit up
    and see the way you're going on's going to make us split up.

CELIA.
    I see, preliminaries over, and now
    the bit you really like. Giving me a row.

ALEX.
    I'm not! Sweetheart, listen! Honey, all I'm saying
    is you're too easy and open with everyone and that's not
                                                        playing
    fair with them, now you're mine, babe, is it?
    I'm crowded out and crushed by every visit –

CELIA.
    Can I help it if you're not the only one to fancy me?
    Should I take a stick and beat them off then? Answer me!

ALEX.
    No need for any stick, but you should make it clear
    that now we're an item they're not so welcome here
    as maybe once they were? Now that we're together
    avoid looks that could be taken as come hither.
    To other men the fact you're unattainable
    will make you even more attractive – if such a thing were
                                                        possible!
    But I don't see you doing anything to dissuade them!
    The way you are with them might just persuade them
    that they're in with a chance still? I know you don't flirt,

but you have to show them you're not some bit of skirt
there for every Tom, Dick or Harry's gratification.

CELIA.
Excuse me?

ALEX.
            Sometimes I think every other bugger in the nation
is after you as well. They are! How could they not be!
Just tell them you're mine and you belong to me
as the old song says – you see how corny
you make me? Bewitched, bothered, bewildered – horny
as all hell too, God help me, and that's the nub
of it. You're gorgeous, Celia, and there's the rub!
I love you so much, darling, surely I deserve
you listen to me and . . . act with more reserve?
For instance, Ceels, why are you so pally
with Clint Andrews, MSP? I'm curious, naturally.
What do you see in him. Give me a hint!
Is it his muscles or his mind? He is some Clint!
When most ex-footballers get dumped by their club
they don't run for parliament, they run a pub!
– Well, there is that prat Vinnie Jones and Hollywood –
But for Clint Andrews it was Holyrood,
Holyrood or bust! That's where Clint Andrews seems to crave
the limelight in Armani and too much aftershave.
He's sunbed-orange Tommy Sheridan perma-tanned,
his teeth are more capped than he ever was for Scotland
and he flashes them in a far too-white inane grin.
Celia, I can't see why you ever let him in –
or the too faithful Scottish public either who couldnae resist
voting for him despite the penalties he missed
in his not entirely glittering international career.
That bastard always seems to be hanging 'round here.

CELIA.
Alex, why must you slag off everyone?
Clint's my friend. He is a lot of fun.
Plus he's in the position to do me a lot of good
with the selection committee. Hello? Holyrood . . .

ALEX.

> Don't suck up to tubes like him. Celia, I'd prefer it
> if you'd trust you'll get selected on your merit.

CELIA.

> Alex, why are you so pathologically jealous?

ALEX.

> Celia, why are you so free with everybody, tell us!

CELIA.

> I'm just the same with everybody. Doesn't that reassure you?
> Accept I'm a *People Person* and it'll cure you
> of this thing of yours. If there was something intense
> between me and one individual it might make sense.

ALEX.

> Maybe I'm just one of your 'people' then!
> What more of you do I get than other men?

> CELIA *sits up and pulls on a flimsy shift:*

CELIA.

> You lie here beside me in my bed
> and say you don't believe the love that we've just made!
> Well done! Your jealousy's resulted
> in the one you say you love being utterly insulted
> What more of me do you get than other men!
> What kind of question's that? Well then,
> get out! Alex, go and fuck yourself, OK?
> I'm no longer going to give this shit the time of day.

ALEX.

> No one ever loved a woman the way I love you!

CELIA.

> You have a novel way of showing it, that's true!
> What's the matter with you, you can't enjoy a
> wee bit of *amore* without possessiveness and paranoia
> when other folk would be happy to settle for a cigarette!
> I let you love me, Alex, and this is what I get?

ALEX.

> The remedy for all this is up to you!
> This carry on only makes us both sad and blue!

Baby, I know how sweet you are – and pure and good
– and I know how easily friendliness is misconstrued.
Let's not fight! But you could try and put a stop –

The doorbell goes.

ALEX.
Ignore it!

CELIA.
                    Archie said he might come up!

*Delighted, she gets up and goes swiftly and easily to answer
the door, revealing she has no pants on as she carelessly
scratches her lower back, then pulls down the flimsy thing
she's wearing. She lifts up the intercom to her ear.*

ALEX.
Don't let him in!

CELIA.
                    Hello?

From the intercom

ARCHIE.
                    It's me!

CELIA.
Archie, darling, just the man I want to see!

*She presses the release button to let him in downstairs and
opens the door too, leaving it ajar.*

ALEX.
Is it an alien concept to you, privacy?
Are you never not at home to company?

CELIA.
I wouldn't want to do anything to offend him.

ALEX.
Tell him you're busy and to bugger off, hell mend him!
He can't help your political aspirations, he's a Green!
And a more effete upperclass wanker, by the way, I've not
                                                    seen!

CELIA.

Are you insane? Don't you know how to network?
You put out feelers, set in motion little things you let work
for you across the party lines, and Arch knows everyone.
It's the age of spin when all is said and done
and Archie's got all the old connections, plus his charm.
He might not be able to do me good but could do harm.

ALEX.

However you rationalise it, what hurts me
is that us being together isn't your first priority
We're busy! Occupé! Can't they take a hint?

ARCHIE *pops his head round the door.*

ARCHIE.

Guess who I met on his way round here? Old Clint!

ALEX.

Oh no!

CLINT *pops his head round the door*

CLINT.

Hi Ceels!

ARCHIE *and* CLINT *both disappear again.*

ALEX.

I'm out of here!

As he goes to throw back the covers CELIA *picks up his
underpants and trousers from the floor.*

CELIA.

I don't think you're going anywhere, my dear!

ALEX.

Why should I stay?

CELIA.

Because I want you to.

ALEX.

No way!

CELIA.

    None?

CELIA throws his pants onto the mantelpiece where they stick, hung up out of reach over an ornament. And chucks his trousers to the other corner of the room.

ALEX.

What difference does it make to you?
They talk such pish! It is a total bore
to stay and listen to the same old shite I've heard before.

CELIA.

All the difference in the world, dear Al!
Stay. I wish to introduce my lover to my pal.

ALEX.

I can't!

CELIA.

    You won't!

ALEX.

    I won't then. Never!

CELIA.

Well fuck off, Alex, then! For ever!

She opens the door looking to see what's holding up the other two.

CELIA.

Guys! Where are you? Aren't you coming in? I'm sorry . . .

ARCHIE.

We're waiting on your stepsister! Ellie, pet, do hurry!
She met your downstairs neighbour on the stair –

CLINT comes in laughing and shuts the door.

CLINT.

He's all over her! She's well in there.

ELLIE opens the door, announces –

ELLIE.

Phil's on his way up, I met him in the Café Royal –

*The trio go straight to the fridge in the kitchen area, begin
to get out a bottle of fizzy and footer with the wire around
the cork.* CELIA *turns to* ALEX.

CELIA.
　Still here?

ALEX.
　　　　　Phil too! Great! Let's not spoil
　the party, oh no, by leaving anybody out!
　The more the merrier! What's open-house about
　at Madam Celia's but welcoming all-comers with
　　　　　　　　　　　　　　　outstretched arms!
　And legs wide-open too, why not! Just share your charms
　with all the world, there's nothing weird about this situation.
　Next time we want to shag let's do it in Waverly Station!
　Suits me, Celia. Them or Me. Before them all today
　you're going to declare your choice. And publicly.

CELIA.
　You are off your head, you very silly man.

ALEX.
　Not at all. Get out of this one if you can.

CELIA.
　I beg your pardon!

ALEX.
　　　　　Choose!

CELIA.
　　　　　You're kidding me!

ALEX.
　I've been far too patient! Now we'll see!

*There is a great laugh from the others who come over to the
bed bringing the bottle and glasses.* CELIA *accepts,* ALEX
glares and declines with a gesture. ARCHIE *begins to roll
a fat joint.*

ARCHIE.
　That prick Parr this afternoon at the Parliament.
　said 'Are you trying to infer ?' when he surely meant

'Are you trying to *imply*'. The man's an ignoramus.
His gaffes of grammar and vocabulary are famous.

CELIA.
Parr's an arse! His error-strewn verbosity
Is a side effect of his penchant for pomposity.
He's that puffed-up the man's a walking joke.
Someone ought to tell him he's a laughing-stock.

CLINT.
Talking of laughs, I vernear pished masel.
Wendy had buttonholed McConnell in the Cowgate and,
                                                    well,
she was giving it chapter and verse and keeping the fella
staunin in the pishin rain withoot an umbarella.

CELIA.
Wendy could talk for Scotland, so she could.
You stand there glazing over, try to listen, for all the good
it does you. It's incomprehensible! Wendy enjoys
the sound of her own voice all right but it's . . . white noise.

PHIL.
Knock, knock!

ELLIE.
                    They're tearing everyone to shreds here, Phil!
Come on in, man, you're missing yoursel!

CLINT.
Quigley seems to be a character. What's his history?

CELIA.
How that prat got where he is is a total mystery.
He never remembers who you are,
ignores you utterly unless you are a media star
who's happened to swim into his orbit so frequently
you've registered. Then it's presumptuous intimacy
with Queen Quigley whispering, to your consternation,
this confidence or that inside information
– 'a wee word in your shell-like ear'
that's how he puts it. He's like: 'My dear,
don't let me interrupt your conversation, *but –* '
then some utterly obvious shite. You're like: *shut*

up, you self important old tosser! But you do your best
to smile, go: 'Really I didn't know that!', act impressed.
Even his 'good morning', his every banality
Is delivered with this same smirk of confidentiality.

ARCHIE.
What about McGillvray Cotter?

CELIA.
                                        That fantasist!
Cotter's top of his own Best-Filmmaker-in-Scotland list!
Not a celeb in Scotland but Cotter will purport
to be a friend of theirs. 'My *project* has support
from a certain Scotsborn filmstar who shall be nameless!'
My arse! He's a namedropping starfucker! He's shameless!

CLINT.
He and Candy Tate are meant to be real close . . .

CELIA.
Candy Tate! On the box she tends to be *verbose*
if anything – let's say she's seldom stuck!
In real life though? Candy – just my luck –
seems to think that she and I are best of pals!
– Well, she's into connections and she knows I'm Al's –
So up she comes, uninvited, just drops in 's
though she owns the place, and, for my sins,
I'm meant to entertain her. Well,
she sits there saying nothing. Clams up. Bloody hell,
every conversational gambit that I try
she drops the ball and lets the whole thing die!
Read any good books, Candy? Nada! She's the pits!
Unbudgeable, though. For hours. Just sits.
The weather, fashion, politics, gossip, culture –
Zilch! Fuck all to say without a researcher
to tell her what to think! I don't want to bitch on
but only in front of the camera does she switch on.

CLINT.
Yon Zoe Thingwy gave her quite a write-up!

CELIA.
The Zoe Arnott Column, yes, well not quite up
my street! Our feminist nationalist commentator –

ARCHIE.

                                        Quite!
What leads that opinionated bitch to think that she can write?

CELIA.

Ego. Ego!

ARCHIE.

                And *what* do you make of Tam Craig?

CELIA.

                                    – So up himself!
Always full of indignation on his own behalf!
Someone else got such and such award
because some enemy on the committee put in a bad word!
Actually, he's done very well indeed, I must say
he's made a very meagre talent go a gey long way!

CLINT.

What about Kit McTavish? He asked us to a party.
Should I go or will it be . . . dead arty?

CELIA.

He splashes out on food and drink, and how!
No one'd go except for the Nick Nairn chow!

ELLIE.

The spread that Kit puts on is ultra-lavish!

CELIA.

But he's a gey queer dish of fish himself, McTavish!
His parties should be great, but, bloody hell,
there's all the extra shit you've got to eat as well!

PHIL.

How about Sir Dugald Scougall? What's your line
on our old boss then?

CELIA.

                Doug's a friend of mine!

PHIL.

Has anyone a bad word to say 'bout him? Never.

CELIA.

– *Except* . . . he annoys me by trying to be clever.
He *is*! That's not something he has to demonstrate

the whole time. I feel like saying: you'd be great,
Sir Dugald, darling, if you'd *relax*. It's such a pain
you won't come down from that elevated plane
you operate on constantly and just *engage*.
Do you good to occasionally get on the same page
as some of us intellectual pygmies! This superior schtik,
this 'nothing pleases me', it makes you look a prick,
quite frankly. He praises nothing, everything fails
by his high standards. Argue and he audibly exhales,
shakes his head as if to say: that's no good I
am utterly unpersuaded by your point, how could I
not let the standard of debate in this place depress me?
He crosses his arms, looks down. He's like: Impress me.

ARCHIE.

That's Sir Dugald Scougall to a tee!

CLINT.

Absolutely, That's just him! Fuck me!

ALEX.

Is anyone left unscathed? I think not!
Everything's rehashed, everyone's trashed by you lot!
But if any of these people were to turn up here
you'd be all over them like a rash. *Criticise*? No fear!
You'd be knocking each other out the road
to kiss their arses, oh, yes you would!

ARCHIE.

Hey, don't get at us, Al. Don't you feel ya
Should . . . perhaps be complaining to your Celia?

ALEX.

No I do not! You bastards are the ones to pander
To Celia's weakness for witticisms, gossip and slander.
She wouldn't do it – approval's what she's after –
deprived of the oxygen of your laughter.

PHIL.

Wait a minute, Alex! You can talk!
I've heard you say much worse about these very folk!

CELIA.

Alex Frew's obliged to be contrary.

If everyone says one thing, he doesn't care, eh?
He'll say the exact opposite, He will!
Automatically, As a matter of principle.
He plain despises others' views, it'd annoy
our Alex far too much to side with the hoi polloi.
Make a statement 'bout someone you've already heard him
                                                    make
and he'll contradict it, for contradiction's sake.
When he hears it come from the mouth of some companion
he'll go back on himself and his stated opinion
and argue the toss with one and all
that that wasn't what he said at all.

ALEX.

Well done, Celia, you've got your audience laughing.
Any more let's-get-at-Alex in the offing?

PHIL.

You are a contrary bugger, but, it's true!
Nobody can say anything about anybody 'cept you.
One minute you're anti praise and flattery and stuff,
next thing you're up in arms someone got slagged off!

ALEX.

When I listen to people I get totally disgusted.
There's smarmy false praise, which isn't to be trusted.
That's to folk's *face*, but behind their back
it's character assasination and malicious attack.

CELIA.

But –

ALEX.

        It kills me. It really does.
They laugh. You show off. It gives them a buzz
to egg you on and generally encourage you
to display the faults for which they secretly disparage you.

CLINT.

Whit faults? Lex, your harsh words reveal ya
urr totally wrong for your woman here, eh Celia?

ARCHIE.

Faults! Am I biased? P'raps I am
but our fair Celia seems perfect, near as damn.

ALEX.
> She's aye struck me as far from same!
> I've made no secret of it. I'm quick to blame
> my darling when she falls short of her lovely best.
> I am! Is that not so, Celia? The acid test
> for true love is that it's not blinded by brilliant sex
> into looking at the one you love through rosy tinted specs.
> You have to be honest with each other, that's what matters.
> The more a lover truly loves the less he flatters.

CELIA.
> Are you listening to Alex one and all?
> Sweet nothings? Sweetie, they're worth sweet fuck all!
> I don't quite get it – but maybe I'm obtuse,
> seems the highest expression of love is dog's abuse!

ELLIE.
> Seems to me that – sorry to be a dissenting voice –
> *au contraire*, lovers always rationalise their choice.
> Passion seldom sees anything wrong at all!
> The lovee's each flaw is a virtue they extoll.
> He deems her 'translucently fair' whom rationally
> you'd call pale and insipid – if not peelly wally.
> She's swarthy, with a dark moustache, and yet
> to the man who loves her she's 'my beautiful brunette'.
> Your anorexic Olive Oil type, skinny as a rake?
> She's 'slender', 'supple', '*graceful*', for goodness sake!
> If she's a big girl – frankly fat as a pig –
> she's 'majestic', she's 'a galleon sailing at full rig'.
> The giant's 'a goddess', the poison dwarf's 'petite'
> If she's a silent halfwit she's 'deep' and 'sweet'.
> The blether is 'vivacious', 'fun', 'good value'.
> – Or that's what her besotted swain will tell you.
> Say a chap takes up with an Older Woman?
> The type the world calls, kindly, 'No Spring Chicken'?
> Her lover says 'sophisticated' 's what is meant.
> Underage? Still wet behind the ears? She's 'innocent.'
> The slattern, the 'careless beauty', the one who begs
> for a bloody good scrub is 'sex on legs'.
> The snob's 'sensitivity' elevates her above the commonality.
> The ill-favoured one has 'a great personality'.

In fact the total dog with no redeeming feature
is said by her beau to have 'the nicest nature'.
Thus does the lover love and the result's
the deification of the loved one's objective faults.

ALEX.
And I maintain that –

CELIA.
                              Yes, we know exactly what you think.

ARCHIE *and* CLINT *look as if they are about to go.*

CELIA.
Chaps, stay! D'you want another drink?
You off?

ARCHIE *and* CLINT.
                    No! No Celia!

CLINT.
                    No way!

ALEX.
Why are you so scared they go away?
Suit yourselves, gents, but be clear
I'm not going to be first to go and leave you here!

ARCHIE.
I've nothing so pressing it urgently deserves
seeing to, unless I'm getting on Celia's nerves?

CLINT.
Until my Surgery tomorrow night, seems to me
there's nothing I have to do that urgently . . .

To ALEX –

CELIA.
You have got to be kidding.

ALEX.
                              But I'm not!
Choose between me and this lot.

The phone rings. CELIA *answers it* (*a corded handset*).

CELIA.
Hello . . . Mhm . . . Mhm . . . Mhm . . . Quite.
Alex, there's a person here to speak to you, alright?

She holds out the handset of the phone, cord stretched, triumphantly, well out of his reach. ALEX is stuck in bed naked.

ALEX.
Tell them to ring me at home. Why here?

CELIA.
I think they know where to find you, my dear.

Waving the phone, she sits down, very legs akimbo, facing upstage, facing ALEX, who is soon ruffled and blinking.

ALEX.
Well give us it!

CELIA.
                    Come and get it.

Through gritted teeth –

ALEX.
I'm stuck here naked!

CELIA.
                    Whoops! How could I forget it?

ALEX.
Jesus, will you give me the bloody phone?
Instead of sitting giving it the Sharon Stone!

CELIA.
Perhaps Clint'll pass you the cordless.
Say pretty please though, not a word less.

ALEX.
Why in God's name should any bugger ring me –
Alright, Clint, go on, pass the thingwy.

CLINT.
Sorry, Lex, I didnae quite catch whit you're sayin . . .

ALEX.

Please! Pass the cordless. Is that plain?

CLINT.

Aye, no bother Alex, there you are.

Celia, d'you want to come out to the Tapas Bar?

ALEX (*on phone*).

Hello. Alex Frew here, speaking.

CELIA.

                                    Naah!

I don't think I'll bother, Clint my sweet, but ta!

ALEX (*on phone*).

Who me? Oh right, right, yes, OK.

He clicks off the phone.

ALEX.

I've to go in and see Sir Dugald straight away.

PHIL.

Alex, I told you –

ALEX.

                         – OK! Pass my pants, Phil. Please.

PHIL.

Where are they?

Through gritted teeth –

ALEX.

                         On the mantelpiece.

PHIL.

On the *mantel* . . . ? Ah! There's your Calvin Kleins.

PHIL picks them up slowly

ALEX.

– Would you give us them for Chrissake, they're mines!

PHIL hands them over.

PHIL.

I suppose it was obvious, I should have seen
this coming . . .

CELIA.

What on earth d'you mean?

PHIL.

Oscar and Alex almost came to blows.
Last night. About some verse of O's.
Al, be conciliatory, please, to the best of your ability.

He's squirming into his pants under the covers.

ALEX.

I take nothing back. I refuse to show servility,

PHIL.

Oscar's father has given you a three line whip.

ALEX *gets out of bed in his underpants and socks, strides
for his trousers, and as he jumps into them, zips up, gets
into his loafers –*

ALEX.

I suppose the *blood's thicker* thing could tip
the balance with Sir Dugald over Oscar's stupid verse?
I'll stick to my guns though, there's nothing worse
than not having courage of one's convictions. I'm not
going back on it supposing Sir Dugald cancels my slot!
I'll say: neither in terms of talent, nor temperament'lly
Will Oscar ever make a poet.

PHIL.

OK, but put it gently.

ALEX.

That so-called poem was absolutely execrable!

PHIL.

Sure, but you have to say it is abominable
In a nice way. C'mon!

ALEX.

I'm going, but it's a disgrace
how just to tell the truth –

PHIL.

Go show your face!

ALEX.
  Sir Dugald'll see how with Oscar there was nothing at all
  I could do except be honest. It's nothing personal!

  To CLINT *and* ARCHIE *who are killing themselves
  laughing.*

ALEX.
  Altruistic of you guys to be scrupulously refusing
  to find the misfortune of others amusing.

CELIA.
  Go Alex!

ALEX.
      In my absence there's no lack
  of company for you, thank God. But I'll be back!

  PHIL*'s at the open door already. Picking up rest of clothes*
  ALEX *exits,* PHIL *following and shutting the door.* ELLIE
  staring after them concerned. CELIA *laughing like a drain
  with* CLINT *and* ARCHIE.

  Black.

  End of Act Two.

  Interval.

ACT THREE

Still Celia's open-plan loft. A little later. CLINT *and* ARCHIE *alone, still sitting it out, each determined not to leave before the other.*

CLINT.

Archie Fairbairn, you really think you're Erchie!
That cool! That posh! That suave! No faur to search, eh,
for reasons to think you're really it? Oh well,
see if you were chocolate, man, you'd eat yoursel.

ARCHIE.

I don't think, objectively, that if I looked in the mirror
I'd see anything to fill me with utter horror.
I'm rich! I'm young! I'm what *you'd* call landed gentry.
– Pied a terre here, stately home in the country.
Myself, I think nothing of inherited wealth and class –
Debretts and *debutantes* can kiss my ass,
quite frankly. I'm confident I'll make it on my own,
that my talent, wit and acumen can stand alone.
I half-own that seafood joint down the shore at Leith
I've got my own hair, I've got all my own teeth,
I've got looks, I've got brains and, though I say it as shouldn't,
the Greens would be nowhere without me, they wouldn't
necessarily have had someone with the *charm* to get elected
so the environment in Scotland would be unprotected –
and the environment is something I'm passionate about.
I'll fight for a Dear Green Scotland, have no doubt!
Now, with a politically-converted Celia by my side –
wouldn't she be the ultimate classy politician's bride?
Picture nuptials on a Scottish island, on the shore
with whale-song for our wedding march and more
tartan-clad guests than Madonna and Guy could rustle
up for their so-called stellar wedding in Skibo Castle.

Picture the driftwood in the flowers, the organic champagne
                                                          flow,
picture the exclusive wedding pictures in Hello!
Oh, and imagine the widespread desolation
among Edinburgh's – no *Scotland's* – female population!

CLINT.
Aye, they are all mad for you. Since you can enjoy as
gorgeous a bit of totty as Celia anytime, away and don't
                                                    annoy us!

ARCHIE.
There are other women, sure, but none that appeals
– and none that I appeal to – quite like Ceels

CLINT.
What about Alex Frew? In her bed there? Hello?
Is she no supposed to be *engaged* to that so-and-so?

ARCHIE.
That is never ever going to last. It
seems that, sexually, Alex Frew is past it.

CLINT.
Really?

ARCHIE.
        Yes. That's what Candy said.

CLINT.
But . . . there he was. Today. In Celia's bed.

ARCHIE.
Means nothing! Cuddle, tea and sympathy.
According to Candy it's not responding to the therapy.

CLINT.
Candy told me. Yeah, I heard that too.
I just wondered whether you actually knew!
Amazing, eh? They don't actually shag?
Bugger me! Has he not tried yon Viag –

ARCHIE.
– Doesn't always work! These things are a mystery.
Candy says Ceels's sorry for him, but, basically, he's history!

CLINT.
> Then you believe, Celia-wise, you are in with a shout?

ARCHIE.
> Of that, dear Clint, I have absolutely no doubt.

CLINT.
> You are utterly deluded there, my son.
> You flatter yourself, you kid yourself on.

ARCHIE.
> I flatter myself, I kid myself, that's true.

CLINT.
> What makes you think Celia'd fancy you?

ARCHIE.
> I flatter myself.

CLINT.
> I mean: based on what?

ARCHIE.
> Ego. Ego. I kid myself.

CLINT.
> What proof've you got?

ARCHIE.
> I kid myself, I tell you!

CLINT.
> Has our Celia
> said anything to make you feel ya
> might be in with a chance wi her, romantically?
> If so, I'll clear the field for you. Fair play!

ARCHIE.
> No. She treats me like dirt.

CLINT.
> Just say!

ARCHIE.
> Like something to be wiped off her shoe.

CLINT.
                                        Away!
Tell me what hope she's dangled afore you?

ARCHIE.
She's turned me down flat. You know the score, you
have much more chance with her than me. If I'd any pride,
integrity or plain courage I'd try suicide.

CLINT.
Suicide my arse! Listen to me man!
Let's agree on this together. Here's my plan:
when one of us is chosen – when and if –
all he has to do is show the other proof
and he'll step aside, throw in the towel, yield
and leave the victor with an empty playing field.

ARCHIE.
Brilliant Clint. I agree. Put it here!
Let's shake on it. A great idea.

The buzzer goes and CELIA *comes in in a bathtowel from
the shower, unconcerned, disinterested, sees them still there.*

ARCHIE.
– Ssh!

CELIA.
        Still here?

CLINT.
                Passion nails us to the flair.

CELIA.
Who the Hell is this now? Hello! Who's there?

ZOE.
It's me! Zoe. Can I come up for a bit?

CELIA.
Darling of course! – *Oh* Shit! Shit! Shit!
What does that dreadful woman want with me?

ARCHIE.
Sweet, I don't think I can bear to wait and see.

CLINT.

    Nor me! Cheeri!

ARCHIE.

               We're off pet! Ciaou!

CELIA.

    What does Zoe bloody Arnott want with me now?
    That fucking prude! That hypocrite!
    Don't leave me!

CLINT *and* ARCHIE.

             By-ee!

CELIA.

             Stay a bit!

But they've gone. A snort of utter exasperation from CELIA.

CELIA.

    Oh! Thanks a bundle you useless pair,
    I'm stuck with Ms. Censorious, but you don't care.
    Zoe Arnott! Deep down she's horny as the next,
    always trying to get her hooks in some poor man on some

                                     pretext.

    It never works! The object of her lust
    is off like a shot, you'll not see him for dust!
    Those of us who *can* pull make our Zoe green.
    She calls normal heterosexuality obscene.
    Yet she's man-mad! She'd love one! Mine!
    She has such an obvious thing for Alex. Fine!
    Pity he finds you repulsive, but on you go, eh?
    Very sisterly to be after my fiancé –

Enter ZOE.

CELIA.

             Zoe!

    Dar-ling! What brings you here?
    I was getting awf'lly anxious about you, dear.

ZOE.

    I thought it my duty to give you some advice.

CELIA.

Darling! Sing up then, don't think twice . . .

ZOE.

I'm glad they're gone!

CELIA.

Me too!

ZOE.

Gives me the chance to speak in confidence to you.

CELIA.

Shall we be sitting comfortably ere you begin?

ZOE.

No need!

I've got something to say to you I hope you'll heed
and – especially – take in the spirit in which it's meant.
Frankness in friendship is a compliment,
yes? Celia, believe me, this is hard for me
And that I pass this on is testament to the intimacy
I feel exists between us? Our friendship's strong
and I simply hate it when people get you wrong.
Well, yesterday, to my consternation
your name came up – unflatteringly – in conversation.
The consensus being that you were somewhat of a slut
who's slept her way to the top, and but
for sex and Sir Dugald Scougall would still be a researcher.
Your journalistic skills were strictly 'Wot-a-scorcher!-'
'Street-of-Fear'-type clichéd tabloid dreck.
– But, you had a flauntable ass and a brass neck.
That was basically it. I defended you vociferously.
They'd know this was very far from true if it was up to me!
I said, maybe she only got a two-two at university
but what does stuff like that matter anyway?
I said Celia does not sleep around so rid
yourself of that notion. Nobody's business if she did
when she was up for a good time, young and single.
She was always scrupulous enough to never mingle
business with pleasure. If you've heard otherwise, it's just

not true!

I said, these days Celia's engaged to Alex Frew

and she's going to deceive him? Yeah, right!
But, when I thought about it, I thought you might
be extra careful not to give the bastards ammunition
and that the smart thing in your situation
would be to simply not be seen with other men?
They couldn't make their nasty innuendos then!
I know if you heed this . . . wee word to the wise
and *think on*, you'll do as I advise.
Believe me, I only tell you this because I care!
My one concern, Celia, is for your welfare.

CELIA.

Don't I know it! Darling! My attitude
to what you've said is nothing but gratitude
and – very far from taking it amiss –
I'm so moved you levelled with me I could kiss
you, honestly. Out of sheer sisterhood
you repeated all that nasty stuff for my own good!
And don't I know it! Did me such a good turn
I really must reciprocate your kind concern.
People talk to *me* of *you*, and I get the feeling
because we've both broken through the glass ceiling –
well, on the face of it, Zoe, we are well-matched.
I'm still young and single and . . . well, you're unattached
and we're both strong successful women who are upfront,
speak out 'bout things – so we're bound to bear the brunt
of the endemic institutionalised misogyny
that is, God help us, *still* our lot today!
They say you're the kind of feminist that fights
in an abstract way for woman's rights
but pays less than minimum wage to her cleaning lady
and treats the poor woman abominably.
Do you know, they call you a prude and make fun
of the fact that you are on your own,
say you're *sour-grapes* anti-sex? And – this is a stumer! –
accuse *you* of that old chestnut: No Sense of Humour.
They say you've no style, dress as though you hate
yourself. I said this is *deliberate*,
you dumbos, so she's taken seriously!
Well, I'm always as quick to defend you as you are me.
To my horror they would have none of it:

you were an opinionated, passremarkable sanctimonious shit.
Well I was hurt for you, then it occurred
that *if* you were to shut up 'bout other's faults you'd render

absurd

any suggestion of piousness or hypocrisy?
Zoe, my darling, it really isn't up to me,
but – I know if you heed this . . . wee word to the wise
and *think on*, you'll do as I advise.
Believe me, I only tell you this because I care!
My one concern, Zoe, is for your welfare.

ZOE.

I've hurt your feelings! Celia, pet, you
know the last thing I wanted was to upset you!

CELIA.

Absolutely! Oh, I know, believe me I do know!
Get out your Filofax, when's your next window?
I think we should make this a regular date.
Let's do this every week. Wouldn't it be great
if we could tell each other what the talk of the town is,
who next we're going to drum out of the feminist brownies
and what the word is about each other on the street?
A Mutual Admonition Society! Wouldn't that be neat!

ZOE.

There's no talk about you. These days I'm the joke.
Feminist principles are a laughingstock.

CELIA.

Feminism-schmeminism! Yeah, 'Mascara's a sin!'
'Men's scum!' 'Sex is Oppression!' That old crap again!
You even tried political lesbianism, why?
It's not in that direction your predilections lie.
Something 'bout sapphism being the way for the radical

feminist?

But you couldn't even get a dyke to jump you, pissed.
So you've embraced the 'new celibacy', are always

lecturing me

on the perils of sleeping with the enemy.
The celibate calls sex a drag – or so I've found –
because her sex-life is a desert she calls the moral high

ground.

I don't mean to piss you off, but, Zoe, I'm afraid,
the New Celibacy is just the old Can't Get Laid.

ZOE.

– Which is not something anyone'd say about you!
Some of these slurs about you are true
and everybody knows it! When I think how I defended
so vigorously someone who could be depended
on to take it all wrong, well I could cry!
Celia, why are you so bloody hostile. Why?

CELIA.

Me! *I'm* hostile! Be a little self-aware.
You openly attacked me. Now, I don't care
though I – marginally – prefer you *passive* aggressive.
Jesus H. Christ, what is so transgressive
about *normal* behaviour, mmm? Like mine?
If men fancy me, they fancy me, fine!
Am I to beat them from my doors?
I'm not stopping you from getting yours.

ZOE.

Do you think I'm interested in your multiple affairs?
Suck all the dick you want. Who cares?

CELIA.

That's nice! Now we have it! Very good!
That's lovely talk. So much for sisterhood!

ZOE.

All this effort to get men to take us seriously
and you just proceed to act outrageously!

CELIA.

I'm sorry! *Effort* to get *men* to *what?*
I must have it all wrong, I thought
feminism was about fighting the good fight
for the assertion of *female* values and our right
to validate *ourselves* and have autonomy.
But it's about what men think of us, I see!

ZOE.

Treat men as sexual objects! That's very liberated!
'Fuck them and chuck them!' Exactly the way we hated

when they did it to us! Role reversal. The *himbo*
to be leched over just like any bimbo.
When women use men, we should equally condemn
the kind of sexual voraciousness we deplored in them.

CELIA.

Oh is that right? Zoe, stuff this puritanical,
No-Sex-Please-I'm-a-Feminist, tyrannical
bullshit right up your ass, why don't you, please!
Just because you're frigid, you want me to freeze!
– Freeze off everyone who makes advances?
Well, I fully intend to take my sexual chances
when I feel like it, and while I'm young!
Men? I like them fit, and hot, and hung!
Got it? OK? And what's that to you?
When did *you* last get a seeing-to?
One knows how much the ageing feminist
deplores the, yes, generally male, amateur psychologist
whose assessment of what she really needs is glib
and that sexual frustration and 'women's lib'
go hand in hand with one another.
But go and get fucked – or alternately don't bother!

ZOE.

I think we better stop before we quarrel.
God knows, I don't see myself as any kind of moral
arbiter, Celia, far from it, Heaven forfend!
Let's bring this ill-starred conversation to an end.
All I wanted was to tell you what people say
so don't shoot the messenger, OK?

CELIA.

I say: why bring the message, Zoe dear?
But, yes, let's put a stop to this right here.
Needless acrimony! Isn't it such a bore?

Enter ALEX.

– and don't go, please! Here's Alex! He'd *adore*
to spend some time with you, don't dash off!
I've got to get dressed and do some stuff –

Alex, look who's here! Your old friend Zoe!
You won't think me rude, Zoe, if I go, eh?

CELIA *exits to bathroom.*

ZOE.
Alex Frew, I'm off in a minute, but how *are* you?
I haven't had a chance to tell you what a star you
are in the new show! It must be up f'r a Bafta, surely?
No-one to touch you, you ought to win it – purely
on merit alone if the world were just.
If! I know a couple of the judges and I must
put in a wee word. I'll do all I can
because, Alex, you know I am your biggest fan.

ALEX.
That's nice you say you like the show. I'm gratified.
As long as the viewers like it I'm satisfied.
Really, Zoe, awards and stuff are neither here or there,
so none of this 'put in a wee word' stuff, don't dare!

ZOE.
All I'm saying, Alex, is I should prefer it
if the Baftas, for once, reflected merit,
rewarded real excellence, gave credit where credit 's due.
If so, TV Personality of the Year would go to you.
So I'll *just* –

ALEX.
                    Good God, are you listening to what I say?
I don't feel undervalued in the industry, OK?

ZOE.
Obviously not, not by those who *know*!
But – Culture and the Arts! – well, it's so
marginal a portfolio isn't it, do you never dream
of doing anything a bit more *mainstream*?
I've written it in my column – and it shouldn't have
                                        surprised you –
that I thought it shameful how *Scotia* under-utilised you
I mean, you could combine what you do now and balance
it with something that would really harness your talents
Something that would carry more –

ALEX.

> Kudos? Fame? I'm not blinking Barrymore.
> Does it not occur to you I'm happy with my niche, eh?
> This is as good 's it gets for me, to use the cliche.
> I need to tell the truth. On my programme I can.
> It might be 'marginal', but I'm my own man.

ZOE.

> I hear what you're saying, I'm going to heed ya
> and drop the whole subject of TV and media.
> I've got to talk to you 'bout – this isn't easy –
> you and Celia, everybody thinks you're crazy.
> Alex dear, you're just not right for one another –
> individually both wonderful, but dis*ast*rous together.

ALEX.

> I thought she was a friend of yours? I'm sorry?
> Between friends bitchiness is mandatory?

ZOE.

> I am her friend, yours too I hope!
> But the ups and downs of your affair make it a soap!
> Yes, a secondhand storyline in some damn soap, a melodrama!
> If I tell you you're betrayed, you'll think I am a
> jealous bitchy person, whereas I'm your true friend.
> Because I know what I know, I know how this will end.

ALEX.

> Nice allegations, you're the betrayer here.
> Of course this sort of stuff's music to any lover's ear!

ZOE.

> She is unfaithful to you, Alex, drop
> her. She does not deserve you, full stop.

ALEX.

> You pay your good friend Celia such a compliment!
> But I don't believe it's entirely kindly meant.

ZOE.

> On the contrary, it is. But if you'd rather ignore
> the truth then, hush my mouth, I'll say no more.

ALEX.

    Whatever. It's up to you, but let me say one thing:
    I wish you'd stop these hints and allegations that don't ring
    true – at all – but spread their nasty little pall of poison
                                 anyway!
    If you have actual proof of something then just say.
    Spit it right out, or for God's sake leave it alone!

ZOE.

    OK: Man we both know has same mobile phone
    as I do. We're at adjoining tables, he picks up
    mine, leaves me with his, innocent mix-up.
    But . . . before we get it sorted – Alex read this text
    then just see what you feel like doing next.

She profers the mobile. He hesitates, then takes it, looks.
Boggles at it, storms out, a 'concerned' ZOE at his heels.

End of Act Three

ACT FOUR

Setting: ALEX*'s flat. A handsome New Town fat. But an unloved, neglected bachelor pad.*

ELLIE BIRD, *in her coat, just recently arrived. and* PHIL, *who has just let her in.*

PHIL.
   He's a stubborn bastard! Every bit of diplomacy,
   every last drop in my producer's armoury
   that's what it took to bring about a reconciliation
   – and not too satisfactory a one either!
   Sir Dugald gave him every chance but he would neither
   apologise to Oscar, nor would be retract.
   He said he stood by everything he'd said and lacked
   any comprehension of why Oscar was offended.
   Said it wasn't as if Oscar's value as a human being depended
   on his ability to write well. Au contraire! It don't!
   He said: I'll call you competent at many things but I won't
   call you a writer! Not by any stretch of the imagination.
   Your free verse was, I'm sorry, an abomination.
   – From which don't infer, son
   it means you're not the nicest person!
   You're both charming and multi-talented by all accounts.
   Clever, I'm sure, but cleverness amounts
   to bugger-all in the making of a poet.
   When one writes that badly the trick is to know it
   and, for one's own sake, to quietly desist.
   You've got cloth ears, so when the Muse tempts, resist!
   All Sir Dugald or I could, with difficulty, achieve
   was that Alex truly wished it had been possible to receive
   Oscar's effort without hilarity, which was rude.
   No one would've been happier than he had it been good,
   he meant this from the bottom of his heart.
   Eventually, they were made to shake on it and part.

Sir D. bade both of us a glacial farewell.
We've not heard the end of this, I can tell!
In the cab back there was the kind of atmosphere I hate.
I was fuming, Alex was in a state,
rushed out to fetch Celia soon as we got home.
Take your coat off, Ellie, wait for him.

ELLIE.

I won't stop, no thank you, Phil
Just popped up to see if the meeting with Sir D. went well.
So – yes and no – he didn't get the sack!
Tell him I dropped in when he comes back.
But, you know, it's rare and admirable, there's such integrity
in such obsessive – often inconvenient – honesty.

PHIL.

Given Alex's nature, you'd think there was gey small
chance the bugger could love anyone at all
– but how did he and Celia find each other?
Ellie, the more I see of the two of them together . . .
well, I can't help but think it strange that a
person like your stepsister should be his inamorata.

ELLIE.

Proves there's seldom a spark between compatible natures?
Maybe they're neither any guarantee of mutual happy futures
nor even any indicator of empathy short term? In fact,
seems it's not just a truism: opposites attract.

PHIL.

He loves her but does she love him back?

ELLIE.

The jury's out on that one. Obviously I lack
First-hand knowledge of the workings of Celia's heart.
Who knows? My stepsister is so very smart
about so much, yet very good at concealing
from her own sweet self exactly what she's feeling.
She'll insist she's immune to someone when she just isn't.
She'll convince herself she loves someone when she doesn't.

PHIL.

He seems pathologically unable to resist her,
but the combination of Alex and your stepsister

is a liaison all too bloody dangerous indeed!
She'll break his heart for him. He'll bleed,
poor bugger! Tell you what I'd do
if I was him, well . . . I'd pick you.

ELLIE.

Don't mock me, Phil. Humiliating enough
that I am the victim of unrequited love.
Is it so obvious? Oh God! I ought to feel such shame
but I love my love with a love that dares to speak its name.
I am – hopelessly – in love with Alex Frew.
He loves my stepsister, I love him. I do.
So much so that actually I hope
Celia loves Alex just as much as the poor dope
loves her, perhaps she really does, and for his sake
I'll dance at their wedding, it'll make
me happy that my darling's happy – pitiful!
Ellie, don't you have any pride at all?
Seems not! Secretly I fantasize
she dumps him, scales fall from his eyes,
he realises he loved me all the time!
And I say yes! Oh yes! – Oh I'm
going to the loo, Phil, excuse me!

Exit ELLIE *to the loo in tears. Alone,* PHIL *berates himself.*

PHIL.

Oh, Ellie! I should've known she'd refuse me
even if I'd managed to actually spit out
what I wanted to ask her. Phil Innes, you great lout!
You wanted to declare your feelings for Ellie Bird
but managed to put it in such a way that what she heard
was you mocking her feelings for Alex Frew!
Feelings that you never – oh, *of course,* you knew! –
but you wanted her to understand old piggy-in-the-middle,
old Phil here, would play second fiddle
and gladly, his dream is to make you his wife!
But did you say it? No. Your whole life
is spent in Alex Frew's shadow, you sad fuck!

Re-enter ELLIE, *composed, from bathroom.*

With brave resolution PHIL *goes to her.*

PHIL.
    Ellie, I –

Enter ALEX *distraught.*

ALEX.
              Philip!

PHIL.
                    – Just my luck!

ALEX.
    Oh Phillip! Oh Ellie, sweet, you must
    help me punish the vile bitch who broke my trust!

ELLIE.
    What is it?

ALEX.
              The world is at an end!
    I'd prefer that than that my Celia, my friend
    and lover, should play me false!
    I'll, I'll – I can think of nothing else

PHIL.
    Now, get a hold of yourself!

ELLIE.
                         Be calm!

ALEX.
    I can't tell you how totally shattered I am!

ELLIE.
    Tell me exactly what she's done?

ALEX.
    Such beauty and such villainy in one?

ELLIE.
    What? And what proved it to you?

ALEX.
    Celia's unfaithful to me! It's true!

ELLIE.
    No!

PHIL.

> Terrible how monstrous jealousy
> breeds nothing but paranoid fantasy –

ALEX.

> Och, away you go and don't annoy a
> man with a broken heart! Proof! Not paranoia!
> Look! Look at this text message!
> Love! Celia doesn't give a sausage!
> A TM to Oscar! Oscar who I'd have voted
> as the guy *least* likely. He was just not quoted.
> Celia! Cheating! And *Who With?*

> ELLIE *takes phone and reads. Her face changes.*

PHIL.

> Alex, there's many an urban myth
> about mobiles and misunderstandings, yeah?

ELLIE.

> Alex, don't go absolutely crazy, eh?

> ALEX *grabs phone back from her. Reads aloud.*

ALEX.

> 'Dear Megashag. Shd v been obvious of course
> You would v been hung like the prvrbial horse
> but 2 cum 5X in 1 night, whod v guessed!
> Quel superstud!!! Im impressed.'

> ALEX *turns to* ELLIE. *Goes right down on his knees.*

ALEX.

> Marry me, Ellie. I mean it. Please!
> Save me from loving Celia, this disease
> I've suffered from for far too long.
> I need someone good and kind and strong
> like you are Ellie. What do you say?
> That would really sicken Celia anyway . . .

ELLIE.

> Believe me, Alex, I have every sympathy
> with what you're going through. Until today
> I'd have thought that I'd have jumped at what you offer.

so lacking in pride – so mad for you – to suffer
the indignity of being *glad* to be your second best.
But it's with a cruel joke you turn to me at last.

Door buzzes. ELLIE *talks to* ALEX *then into door entry
phone. To* ALEX –

ELLIE.
Guess who? (*Into phone.*) Hello?

CELIA.

Ellie*?* It's me!

What are *you* –

ELLIE *presses release to allow entrance then puts front
door ajar.*

ELLIE.

Come up and see!
Alex, if I was to take you on – as if!
I'd only be dumped when you resolved your tiff.
Sicken Celia? You've made me sick!
Oh you'll forgive your Celia again, be thick
enough to believe whatever lame excuse
she comes out with. What's the use
of getting involved with lovers and their quarrels?
Today Celia's a proven slut with the morals
of an alley cat, but, oh, there's something about her
that'll have you apologising you could ever doubt her!
You'll swallow some implausible self-defence
that'll convince you of her charming innocence.

ALEX.
I won't! I won't! This time it's too much!
We are finally through. Never, never, such
appalling, unforgivable behaviour! I'd have to be insane
to ever have anything to do with her again.

Enter CELIA. ALEX *puts his arm round* ELLIE –

ALEX.
Your stepsister here's done me the honour –

ELLIE *shrugs him off, horrified.*

CELIA.

Yeah, to take a responsibility like you upon her
shoulders, Alex, she looks that stupid, I think not!
What's going on now, what's all this lot?

ALEX.

God help, me or I'll swing for you –

CELIA.

Oh God! What did Zoe say to you
that there you stand, eyes blazing with passion
having stormed off in that ridiculous fashion?

ALEX.

Of all the vile things of which a human being is capable
nothing is as bad as what you've done, as damnable
a betrayal as any I've heard of! No one as evil
and as heartless as you, you beautiful devil!

PHIL *signals to* ELLIE *and they sneak off chummily, exit
together, during next.*

CELIA.

Well, Al the Drama Queen, is this not lovely patter?

ALEX.

Don't jest! This is no laughing matter!
Bitch! You should blush to the roots of your being.
I've got proof of all those things I've been seeing
all too clearly but telling myself that I was wrong.
You've been cheating on me all along!
I knew it, I knew it, despite your expertise
with all your lying, cheating ways.
Sex? People just do what they feel like, now.
Love? There is no power, per se, in a vow.
It's a spontaneous thing, love, you can't will it.
The heart cannot be forced, but still it
seems to me you have done me wrong
in so heartlessly stringing me along.
Because, did I tie you up? Excuse me?
Were you *compelled* not to refuse me?
Celia, you could have turned me down

and, without blackening your name all over town,
– oh, hurt, sure! – I'd have accepted it.
No harm to you if you had rejected it,
my foolish heart, just said *no thanks* – God knows
all I could have said was: that's how it goes.
But you lied to me and led me on, said yes.
– Is there no end to your wickedness,
your treachery, falseness, foulness, no?
I'm a man possessed, I'm incandescent, so
just you watch yourself, be very afraid! See you –
I'll, I'll – I can't answer for what I'll do!

CELIA.

What's all this you're making heavy weather
of now? Have you lost it altogether?

ALEX.

Lost it? Yes, Celia, I've lost the lot.
I've lost my life, I've lost my love – I lost the plot,
lost it big time, when I fell hook, line and sinker!
You should be a lovely person, don't you think, or
are your so, so lovely looks just skin deep?

CELIA.

What treachery, Alex? Before you make me weep?

ALEX.

Weep you two-faced, two-timing little bitch!
Read this! Zoe gave me something which
even you can't talk your way out of, dear!
Admit it! You are in it up to here!

CELIA *reads the text in silence. Then she bursts out
laughing.*

CELIA.

So *this* is what has pissed you off?

ALEX.

Does nothing make you blush? Isn't this enough?

CELIA.

Should I be blushing? Tell me why?

ALEX.

You brassnecked wee bizzum, are you going to try
and kid me on you never wrote this text *billet-doux*?

CELIA.

Course I wrote it, and what's that to you?

ALEX.

You sent Oscar *this* – What's that to *me?* –
and you can look at what you've done with equanimity?

CELIA.

For God's sake, Alex, you are such a clown!

ALEX.

No longer! You're going to try and face it down,
this *proof* that you've been shagging Oscar Scougall!
Oscar of all folk! Oh yes, don't try and wriggle
out of this one.

CELIA.

                    This means I slept with Oscar?

ALEX.

Zoe gave me Oscar's mobile. Just ask her!
God, even if you'd written it for some other guy
it'd break my heart – but *him*. Oh why, oh why,
if you must cheat, must you do it with my enemy?

CELIA.

You'll make me piss my pants! He does not fancy me!
Oscar! Please! Nor I him, do you mind?
Surely you've noticed he's quite the other way inclined?

ALEX.

Oh very good! Now Mr. Megashag's a poof?

CELIA.

Of course he's gay! This is not proof
that *he* and *I* are – oh, give me strength!
Matchmaking! I admit I went the length
    of telling Oscar that young David fancied him.
Young David in my office? Alex, don't be dim!
Young Dave the Boy Researcher? Camp as Chloe!
Him you said was dead annoying, oh you know, eh,

and I accused *you* of being a homophobic bastard?
Blond, six-pack, good researcher, keen as mustard!
*Any*way young David declared he had a pash
for my gay pal, Oscar. Let Auntie Celia give it a bash
I said, I'll drop the hint that you are . . . not averse.
I said to Oscar: how 'bout Dave, you could do worse?
Upshot? Off they get with one another.
Clicked. The whole ploy worked, no bother.
Last night's the big date, David comes in, regales
the whole office this morning with the intimate details.
The full bhoona! Who put what, where, when,
how many times, what next. And then . . .
Total blow-by-blow account! We're all like: Woh,
young Dave, more than we need to know!
It was a scream! I texted Oscar on behalf
of the entire office, for a laugh!

ALEX.
Do you think I came up the Clyde on a fucking bike?

CELIA.
Believe me or don't believe me, as you like.
Look at that text again. This is how a screamer
like David talks about sex. You don't dream, or
do you, that women can make love and then
talk that frankly – no, that *crudely* – 'bout men?

ALEX.
Do you really think I'm quite that gullible?

CELIA.
I don't care. I think it's truly terrible
you doubt the woman you said you loved.
You neither loved me nor trusted me, that's proved.

ALEX.
All you have to do is show me how each
word of that vile text is Dave's reported speech –

CELIA.
I won't. It isn't. That was all bullshit.
I'm shagging Oscar blind. I won't pull shit
like that on you – wake up and smell the coffee.

Get mad! Get even! Yeah, break it off, eh,
why don't you, if I'm such a total slag.
Get out of here before I lose the rag!

ALEX.

Could a finer form of torture be invented?
Was ever a heart so deliberately tormented?
I'm justly angry, but when I say so she abuses me,
she turns the tables and accuses *me*
then pushes my suspicions to the limit,
says I'm right, she does me wrong, glories in it!
It's like the old song says, Celia, it's true –
I hate myself for loving you.
That's right! Admit your transgression
with this sarcastic mock confession.
Lay it on thick, as if if you do so enough
I won't realise that it's a double bluff!
Just explain to me what you meant
about this text message being innocent.
What word exactly, what phrase, what bit
and – I'm a sucker for you Celia – I'll swallow it?
Yes, say anything to convince me you're faithful, pretend
and Celia's sad wee clown will buy it in the end.

CELIA.

You're mad. You say you love me to bits
and then subject me to your wild and jealous fits.
I can't believe you had the nerve to ask me to explain
and that I wasted my time in doing so. It's plain
you never loved me or I would have been trusted.
I'd just *tell* you had you been ousted
in my affections. What, I repeat,
is there in it for me, Celia, to cheat?
I've *declared* myself. Alex, we made it official.
I really thought that I had found something special.
But you, you bastard, throw it back in my face,
spy on me, suspect me, doubt me, it's a disgrace
how you treat someone you're supposed to care for.
I should find someone else who'd be there for
me and me alone. Yeah, I *will* find someone new
and all your paranoid fantasies will come true.

ALEX.

> You bitch of Hell! I'm, poor sad fucker,
> stuck with loving you, your sucker
> for the duration until you, somehow, set me free.
> I wouldn't wish a love like this on my worst enemy.
> I'll love you to the bitter end, I'm fated
> to weather the storm of loving you with a love that's unabated.

CELIA.

> No, you don't love me like you should.

ALEX.

> I love you far, far too much for my own good
> and don't I know it? I even wish, fool that I am,
> you were nothing in this world, because if, poor lamb,
> you were not a celebrity, were unvalued, obscure
> I could save and elevate you with my love so pure.
> Ludicrous isn't it? A cosmic joke.
> God must be laughing fit to choke.

The phone rings.

CELIA.

> You wish I was *nothing*! That's excellent.
> Your benevolence I'm sure is kindly meant!
> If I was a carpenter and you a sodding lady!
> Well, I wouldn't love you one bit I'm afraid. – Eh?
> Aren't you going to answer that bloody phone?

ALEX.

> No I'm not. OK? Leave it a-bloody-lone.

Phone answers automatically.

ANSWERPHONE VOICE OF ALEX.

> Leave a message!

ANSWERPHONE VOICE OF ALEX.

>   Al! Alex, pick up for Godssake.
> I know you're there! Celia! Will you make
> Alex pick up, it's bloody urgent, OK?

CELIA *snatches phone up, hands it to* ALEX *who speaks, listens appalled, speaks grunts again.*

ALEX.
Phil? (*Listens.*) Mmhm?

CELIA.
What does he say – ?

ALEX.
Sssh! (*Beat.*) They what? (*Listens.*) They . . . ? (*Listens.*)
Right . . . ?
Yeah (*Listens.*) Yeah (*Listens.*) Mmhm.

Abruptly he hangs up phone, stands shattered.

CELIA.
You're as white
as a bloody ghost, Alex. Tell me what is wrong.

ALEX.
The police have . . . seized my computer, and they'll be along
just directly to nab me too. I've to get my ass over to
Scotia HQ
where they've a lawyer ready to give me a talking to
about saying nothing . . .

CELIA.
Nothing about what?

ALEX.
God knows. I can't think what they think they've got
on me. Some trumped up carry-on, some rammy – ?

CELIA.
Christ Alex! It all sounds very *Get Beltrami* . . .
What is it? Alex, don't be so mysterious!

The doorbell goes. They look at each other in horror.

ALEX.
I don't know what it is – but, Celia, it's serious!

End of Act Four.

ACT FIVE

Setting: CELIA*'s home again. A week later.* ALEX *is packing up the things of his that have found their way to* CELIA*'s.*

ALEX.

I've told you, that's it. I've made up my mind.

PHIL.

I know it's been a blow, but *don't*! I think you'll find –

ALEX.

I'll find fuck all. Don't waste your breath, Phil, please!
The world's a vile place, ambition's a disease,
people constantly do each other down, there is endemic
corruption in the law, the press and politics. Lying's epidemic,
rumours are rife, the papers print filth without consideration
for any individual whatsoever without corroboration
of any kind at all because meretricious gossip sells.
Look at how I've been pilloried for nothing! It smells!
Malicious accusation given credence by a force who can't
be annoyed
to go *wait a minute* before indulging the *schadenfreude*
of the public by announcing that they're questioning me
over allegations of sexual assault they're taking seriously!
Seizing my computer to check for kiddie porn! Oh yes!
Unbelievable! Oh, eventually that lad did confess
he made the whole thing up, a total tissue of lies
– but not before the police checked out my alibis
for all the times the sordid events were meant to have
occurred.
They checked it out, they didn't take my word!
When I was supposed to have been abusing him most
viciously
I was in bed with Celia – hell, you all saw me! –
and you all had to make a public statement to that effect.

Under these circumstances, how can I protect
the remnants of what I laughingly called my privacy.
Is nothing sacred? Is there something wrong with me
that I think some things are no one's business but the
                                        participants?
I blame the politicians. In this, the age of spin, the public
                                        wants
their blood, their guts, gruesome press conference true
                                        confessions
of financial shenanigans and extra-marital indiscretions –
at least the ones that might come out some day!
So it's *let's detonate the ticking bomb and make it go away!*
I had high hopes for a new Scotland and that Holyrood
might say enough is enough, and for the public good
refuse to pander to the lowest or grub after power at any cost.
Once I had high hopes indeed – but now they're lost.
Forever! That's it! I have simply had it up to here
with this place, with the *media*, with the world's gowd and
                                        gear.
I'm getting out! I mean it! Career over! It's no loss!
I've taken a lease on a cottage in Wester Ross.

PHIL.

Don't you think you're being a bit previous? Al, please
don't hotfoot it to the windswept bogs and trees
on account of a storm in a teacup like that.
The general public knows exactly where you're at
and no one believed these allegations for a minute.
It was obvious there was nothing in it!
The Edinburgh and Lothians Constabulary
will no doubt issue you a full and public apology
when they state that you will face no charges whatsoever –
Oh, Alex, I admit it! It wasn't very clever
of them to not send that crazy damaged junkie packing.
He'd tried it on before on other celebs – slander lacking
any substance at all, clearly his deranged and deluded
poor-little-abused-me fantasies everyone, the police included,
knew were utter bollocks but they had to be seen to investigate.
– Once Oscar tipped off the press at any rate.

ALEX.

Coming out in my support! Oscar! That little shite!
'*Never a whisper in media circles!*' He fanned the flames
all right
with his '*everyone at Scotia Television is sure it's utter
malicious nonsense and this rent-boy's a nutter.*'
Why couldn't he do like Sir Dugald and shut his trap?
Because he got his name in the papers spouting supportive
crap
looking good and true and loyal to me in Joe Public's eyes –
and being seen to have been *right* to be so! Big surprise!
The world's gone mad. The human race has lost the plot.
Can you blame me for being pig-sick of the whole damn lot?

PHIL.

I guess not, but –

ALEX.

– *But* bugger-all!
There's nothing you can say in defence of it at all.
After what I've been through in this past week
anything good you can come up with will be pretty unique.

PHIL.

Alex, I'm not going to insult you with some platitude
about there being a lot of good in the world, but your attitude
that the only response to universal wickedness is flight
– well, that's not like my old Alex, that's not right!
Of course the world's a sewer and I'll concede
men ought to act differently. They're very bad indeed.
Expose them! Show them up! For a moral iconoclast
a whistleblower, a scourge like you the scope is vast
because vileness only gives you something to excoriate!
If the world was a nice place how could we appreciate
how Alex Frew the virtuous stood out from the herd?
Listen to me – I'll make sure you hear my every word!
Alex, my point is this: the moral sense
in a wicked world is the perfect defence.
But in the desert, in the empty countryside – how come
you don't see virtue's wasted in a moral vacuum?
There is nothing *there* for you, Al, and you know it!

ALEX.

> I'm going to retire to the country and be a nature poet!
> Your elaborate arguments, Philip, cut no ice.
> Not with me these days. So stuff your advice,
> I've heard it, but my mind's made up, that's it!
> I've burned my boats, resigned. Oh yes, I hit
> Sir Dugald with the news that I was for the offski. Great!
> Now he can piss the whole series away on Candy Tate!
> I said: *Candy Tate interviews the poet Oscar Scougall*'d
> be an excellent first prog of the series, Sir Dugald!
> She's welcome! But, oh Phil, my Celia must agree,
> if she loves me, to up sticks and come up North with me.
> I'll go alone – or Celia and I will go together.
> I'm staying here till I know one way or the other.

PHIL.

> Don't sit in the gloom and wait for her with that glowering
> > face.
>
> Leave a note and come with me to Ellie's place!

ALEX.

> I'm too upset! I'm all churned up inside you know!
> I can't just *socialise*! Go on, away you go
> and leave me with my black despair in this dark corner.

PHIL.

> Sit and feed your huffy wee black dog then, Mister Horner!
> It'll keep you all the company you need – I'm no jealous!
> Bye! I'll not ask you again to come *on*, with me – to Ellie's?

No response. Exit PHIL.

A great loud sigh from ALEX. *It darkens. After a moment,*
without seeing him there, OSCAR *and* CELIA *enter*

OSCAR.

> Yes, yes, Celia, I think it's very commendable
> that you didn't want Alex to feel expendable
> while he was in the middle of a public scandal.
> To get chucked then would've been hard for him to handle.
> But, Celia, sweet, I want to marry you –
> what do you *mean* you don't know what to do?
> Break it off – that's what has to happen next!

Poor old Alex, but I'm *glad* he saw that text!
Well, where you're concerned he's . . . somewhat saft
but now he knows the truth about us, he's not daft!
It's not possible he thought it innocent! It isn't!
Don't let him delude himself – the poor bugger doesn't
know where he is with you! God, I know how he feels!
Give him his marching orders! Pronto, Ceels!
For God's sake! Does he need you to draw him a map?
Ditch Alex – put him out of his misery, poor sap!

CELIA.

Why so down on Alex? What is this?
When once the sun shone out of his every orifice?

OSCAR.

Why do you need an explanation?
I'm simply sick of this stupid situation.
You've got to choose, who's it to be?
Decision time, Celia? Him or me?

ALEX speaks from his gloomy corner.

ALEX.

Well, well! So this is what we find?
The Oscar you said was *quite the other way inclined.*

They gasp and jump back. But ALEX *stands up into the light and quite coolly –*

ALEX.

He's right. You must decide
Which one of us can call you *my future bride*?
You've messed around for long enough, you've got
to shit, Celia, yup – or get off the pot.

OSCAR.

Charming! Well, at least this forces us to have it out.
I have nothing *personal* against you – don't shout!

ALEX.

Who's shouting? Time is up, that's true!
Believe me, I'm not about to share Celia with you.

OSCAR.

If she should prefer your love to mine –

ALEX.

If she chooses you rather than me – well fine!

OSCAR.

– I'd leave and, I tell you, I'd not look back!

ALEX.

I'd harden my heart against her and not crack!

OSCAR.

It's her decision! Tell him, Ceels!

ALEX.

It's not as if she doesn't know exactly how she feels.

OSCAR.

Yes. All she has to do is say!

ALEX.

Absolutely! Then the one who loses will be on his way!

OSCAR.

It's up to her. She has to make her choice.

ALEX.

What's up bitch? Have you lost your voice?

She opens her mouth, but there is a ring at the door. So she goes with relief and alacrity to the entryphone.

CELIA.

Hello?

ELLIE'S VOICE.

Celia? It's Ellie, OK? It's Phil and I.

CELIA.

Come up!

CELIA *opens the door leaves it ajar.*

ALEX.

Oh fucking *great!*

OSCAR.

Ceels, *why?*

CELIA.

I don't see why I should be stranded here with you two
– who seem to be determined to give me a talking to
as if I was some kind of naughty child!
I'm a grown-up woman and I'm getting pretty riled,
to say the least, at being crudely pressurized!
I want out of this stupid situation, are you surprised?
I know which of you I love. Of course I do!
And that person, in his heart of hearts, he knows it too!
But to expect me to speak out before the other and, unabashed,
give him the satisfaction of witnessing the other's hopes
                                                    dashed?
I call that needlessly cruel – I won't do it.
This situation demands we bring some manners to it!
If I have to hurt someone, he deserves the consideration
of being rejected in a *private conversation*!

OSCAR.

No no. Tell me straight. I can stand it.
I want your answer, now!

ALEX.

                    And I demand it.
The truth from your own lips, Celia Mann!
Hurt the loser all you like. Speak up! You can!
You must! There is no need of softening the blow!
We've both told you. Come on! We want to know!
You bitch. You've cheated on us both.
If you care one bit for either, now you'll tell the truth!

OSCAR.

I'll back you up in every way, Sir!
I totally agree with every word you say, Sir.

CELIA.

Yes, terrific, gang up on me why don't you?
Why should *either* of you think I want you?
You're bullies, both of you, bad as each other
Why don't you two go off and get drunk together?
Weep, wail, drown your sorrows, do male bonding
agree women are all bitches, have yourselves a happy
                                                    ending –

ELLIE and PHIL *enter with* ARCHIE, CLINT *and* ZOE *behind them.*

Fantastic! You're all here! The lot! Hello, eh?
Not just Phil and Ellie, but Archie, Clint and Zoe!
Hi! How are you? In you all come, sally forth,
tally-ho, chip in with your tuppenceworth!
These two are persecuting me! Make them desist!
Ellie, they're in cahoots with one another to insist
I've to tell them to their faces, straight,
which one I truly love, which one I hate!
Should I tell them who I'll have and who I'll banish utterly?

ELLIE.
You're speaking to the wrong person asking me!
I'm for one hundred per cent frankness, in no doubt
that I'm on the side of those that favour speaking out!

OSCAR.
Simple. Him or me? No or yes?

ALEX.
See! It's not an option, this evasiveness!

OSCAR.
You have simply got to tell me Celia, I insist!

ALEX.
Just let this appalling silence persist –

OSCAR.
One word, Celia, that is all I need.

ALEX.
– and your saying nothing will be eloquent indeed.

ARCHIE.
Celia, Clint and I – well, we two
have come to pick a bone with you.

To OSCAR *and* ALEX –

CLINT.
Just as well yous guys are here
Affects you too, as we'll make very clear.

ZOE.

    Celia, my pet, it must be a surprise
    to see me back again so soon. I realise
    well, darling, our last meeting – it was not,
    in terms of amicability, perhaps, too hot?
    But these guys came to me, don't think me rude,
    but they are the reason that I intrude
    because what they told me – well, it can't be true
    and I feel it is my duty to help them sort it out with you.
    Oh fuck it! Dear Celia, I thought it'd be such fun
    to see how you get yourself out of this one . . .

ARCHIE.

    Yeah, it's a bloody good one right enough.
    You sent Clint an e.mail, and, here's the laugh,
    my pal here printed a copy out, for me.

CLINT.

    – Well, Archie'd already shown me *this* you see!
    The note you sent him, what do you think?
    Recognise it? Recycled paper, violet ink?

ARCHIE.

    No doubt you'll be familiar with her breezy tone
    I'm sure that Clint and I are not alone
    in receiving Madam Celia's little *billets doux*.
    But perhaps some of this will be news to you?

*(He reads.) Clint, you are talking rubbish when you say
I have any fun at all when you are not here. Your company
is the only real bellylaugh I get and you have kept away for
far too long. Try and come without Archie for a change, he
sticks to you like velcro because I think somewhere deep
down in the dim recesses – and when it comes to Archie
I do mean dim – he does realise you and I have a thing for
one another. (Remember Harris?). Archie never seems to
twig when he's not welcome does he? Yahs like him are
tiresome except in very short doses, but, oh boy, he has such
a big hit for himself that he seems to imagine I have a soft
spot for him. As if! Alex is driving me demented these days,
well this ridiculous business with the police just confirms
his black view of the world. He's been right all along,*

*etcetera. Well, normally sourpuss's tirades do amuse me,
but this time it's getting to be too much. As for young Oscar,
the more I try and shake him off the more he adores me.
Naughty Celia, one trifles with the young at one's peril.
Their energy and enthusiasm are very endearing, not to
speak of their stamina, but one never knows when they are
going to get all serious, send embarrassingly excessive
bouquet upon bouquet from the florist, write one reams of
appalling purple poetry –*

CLINT.

OK, Airch, I think we get the picture. Now for me.
A short extract of *this*, from paragraph three.

(*He reads from a different piece of paper.*) *Why pretend,
Archie, that you are jealous of Clint Andrews? Clint! We go
way back and there is some residual fondness there, on his
part anyway. But nobody in their right mind could take a
clown like him seriously. I don't.*

Is that no hellish? What a fucking cow.
I'm away to tell the world what like she is. And how!

CLINT *goes.*

ARCHIE.

I could say something, but no, I'll not attempt
to explain how far you are beneath my contempt.
Now I'm sure I'll find a sweeter, more faithful match.
Plenty who'd find Archie Fairbairn quite a catch!

ARCHIE *goes.*

OSCAR.

I'm shattered. Celia, this can't be right!
Not after you and me and that fantastic night –
I know you said it was just a bit of fun
but I didn't think you – with just *anyone*?
I see it in your eyes. Oh well, don't vex
yourself about me, you were right, just sex
that's all it was, yes, it was, for me too!
You told me so, I should've believed you.
I won't stand in your way, Alex, now this *hoor*'s
revealed herself for what she is. She's all yours.

OSCAR *goes.*

ZOE.

Well, I've never heard such appalling thing before!
What a shameful story! I'm shocked to the core
Celia, I'm flabbergasted by your lack of morals.
Though I'm not one to mix myself in other folk's quarrels
this time I'm afraid I must speak out.
To reward his love like that? What's that about?
This poor deluded man, he worshipped you
yet –

ALEX.

      Zoe, shut your interfering mouth, please do!
Don't trouble yourself unnecessarily about us.
Your opinions on the matter are superfluous.
I can't pay you back for championing me. Don't bother!
If ever I revenged myself by choosing another –
well, please don't think that because you will stick
up for me that you'd be who I'd pick.

ZOE.

What'd make you think I held a torch for you?
Ego! Ego! And that you have, oh, in spades too!
I'd have to be *beyond* desperate for a lover
to interest myself in Madam Celia's pitiful leftover.
You must be joking. Such as you? For such as I?
Dream on! Yes, that *will* happen! *Why?*
Actually, I hope you sort it out and get together.
For, Alex, you and Celia? You deserve each other!

ZOE *goes.* ALEX *takes a deep breath.*

ALEX.

Well, I've held my wheesht throughout this exposé
And let every other bugger have his say.
Have I exercised sufficient self control?
Now may I –

CELIA.

      Say anything you like at all.
You have every right to reproach me and complain
how badly I've used you. Why? I can't explain.

I'm in the wrong. One hundred percent.
I won't insult you by saying that I never meant
to hurt you – though I did not, that's true.
The anger of those others? I despise it.
But, t'wards you, it's guilt I feel, I recognise it.
Total guilt and shame. Nothing I can expect
but that I've forfeited both your love and your respect.

ALEX.

I ought to hate you! Oh yes! Do I? Oh how
to harden my heart against you, even now?
My head says hate you, but I have to say
my foolish, foolish heart will not obey.

To Phil and Ellie –

You see the bondage and slavery that men call love?
Witness the degradation I can't get free of.
Abject irrational longing, shame, disgrace –
how pitiful the passions of the human race.
Celia, is there nothing you can do
that'll free me from the tyranny of loving you?
Seems not! I forgive the faithlessness
if you'll be faithful from now on. Say yes!
Oh, but you're a bad, bad bizzum, perfidious,
the burden of those letters was unambiguous!
But I forgive you, I forgive you if only you'll agree
to avoid temptation and live quietly with me
in the depths of the country far from humankind –
for I'm in retreat from the world, I've made up my mind.
Let's turn over a new leaf, marry me!
Make it legal, Celia. Holy matrimony!
– and marriage means you are to – understand? – forsake
all others, STOP SHAGGING PEOPLE, OK? FUCK'S SAKE!
Stop! oh, i'm sorry Celia! for what it's worth,
I humbly ask you to marry me and come with me, up north.
Only among wild, sublime and trackless nature
do you and I, Celia, have any future.

CELIA.

My sparkling little light should be hidden
in the dark depths of the country under a midden?

ALEX.

    I love you Celia – and if you loved me too
    Nothing else in all the world would matter to you.
    We'd be all-in-all to one another.

CELIA.

    I'll marry you! Let's move in together!
    We'll sell this, do a big makeover job on yours – en*suite*
    maybe a *mezza*nine, *terrazzo* the – ?

ALEX.

                            – Celia, I repeat,
    I've taken a lease on a remote cottage in Wester Ross!
    Marry me and come with me! Now! Or . . . it's your loss.

CELIA.

    You want me to – run it by me – live up there among the
                                      sheep?
    Can't do it. Sorry, Alex, I'm not that deep.

ALEX.

    Neither you are! You're not. I finally see
    through you. Thank you! You've set me free.
    Loathing has replaced love's pathetic persistence.
    You're not willing to make me your whole existence
    as I'd have made you mine. I did offer. To be my wife
    ought to've been enough! Me – plus a quiet life.

*CELIA pauses and with courage and regret, finally shakes
her head a tight lttle nod, then turns away from ALEX. He
turns to ELLIE.*

ALEX.

    Ellie, I much admire you and hope you can forgive
    me, fool that I am, for my behaviour, crass and insensitive
    to you and your feelings towards me as it undoubtedly was.
    When I asked you to marry me that was because
    Celia's treachery had been revealed in all its hideousness.
    Had you accepted me then it would have been a mess –
    I promise you it would – and, in truth, I didn't mean it
                                     seriously.
    It was a rhetorical proposal. Selfish idiot that's me!
    But forgive me, lovely Ellie, if I do not renew
    my offer of my hand in marriage to you –

I'm not worth it, sweet, so don't you grieve.
Marriage is not for me, I firmly believe.

ELLIE.

Have you taken some sort of funny turn?
Bit late, but yes, I'm glad of your concern,
apology accepted. It's OK, I don't love you any more
that horse has long bolted, don't footer with the stable door.
Phil here and I have a certain ceremony to arrange.
Yes! I'm to be Mrs Phillip Innes, all change!
We want our friends at the wedding, so let's go invite 'em.
Alex, didn't you even notice we'd become an item?

PHIL.

Yes, let's go, Ellie. I've a career to resuscitate.
Alex will do what Alex has to do, that's great.
I've wasted far too long already doing what I can
to hinder the self destructive excesses of this man.

PHIL and ELLIE leave. After them ruefully –

ALEX.

Go Phil and Ellie, I wish you all the best.
Phil, you've got a cracker there – a cut above the rest.
She's a great girl, a shining soul, yup, I think so!
– But, hell, don't ask me, what do I know?

*ALEX surveys the back of the resolute CELIA. She doesn't
look round. He picks up his packed case, announces –*

ALEX.

I'm off out of this cesspit of a city.
Farewell cruel world, and the world's cruel pity!
It's people that are poison. I'll disappear without trace
to somewhere utterly unpopulated – to a place
where liberty of the tongue and truth hold sway
and an honest man can find freedom. I'm away.

*With a little final chink, he puts his keys down on her table
and goes, shutting the door behind him, leaving CELIA
alone. She looks up, genuinely devastated, mouths silently
his name and slumps in hysterical and abandoned weeping.*

Fade to black. End.

TARTUFFE

a translation/adaptation into Scots

for
Marion Keddie
Eleanor Aitken
and the entire Lyceum Company
with love and thanks

Tartuffe was first presented on 24 January 1986 at the Royal Lyceum Theatre, Edinburgh. The cast was as follows:

PERNELLE	Anne Myatt
ELMIRE	Sarah Collier
DORINE	Juliet Cadzow
MARIANE	Gerda Stevenson
CLEANTE	Graham Valentine
ORGON	Stewart Preston
VALERE	Alan Cumming
TARTUFFE	Andrew Dallmeyer
LOYAL/ OFFICER	Billy McElhaney

Director   Colin MacNeil and Ian Wooldridge

Designer   Colin MacNeil

Characters

PERNELLE

ELMIRE

DORINE

MARIANNE

CLEANTE

ORGON

VALÈRE

TARTUFFE

LOYAL/OFFICER

OPENING

When the audience comes in FLIPOTE *and* DORINE *are in the lobby of* ORGON*'s substantial townhouse. There are various doors off it, at least one ajar with a big slice of light cutting from it and occasional flurries of piano music, movement, and laughter spilling from offstage to where in the (almost) darkened hallway, our very bored* MAIDS *smoke on the fly, do up each other's hair into the back of their caps, peek into the offstage party, dare each other to drink some dregs from the removed sherry tray, play cards, yawn out over the audience etc.*

Suddenly the hall light is snapped on with a blaze and PERNELLE *screams on, snapping at* FLIPOTE *to help her into her good winter coat, followed hotly by* ELMIRE *who is a beautiful, worldly, pragmatic, well-dressed, slightly superior mature beauty with a sense of high irony and style.*

Then enter smirking MARIANNE *and* CLÉANTE *. It is a mad dance,* PERNELLE *turns first on one, then the other.*

ACT ONE

Scene One

PERNELLE.
C'moan, Flipote, afore Ah get masel' inty a state.

ELMIRE.
I can't keep up, you're going at such a rate!

PERNELLE.
Wait, haud oan! I've had an ample sufficiency
Of your good manners, there's no necessity –

ELMIRE.
Only nice to be nice, and, on the contrary
As my mother-in-law you're at least due civility.
But why so het-up, Mither, where's the hurry?

PERNELLE.
Ah've to let this rammy a' go by me and no worry?
The wey you clan cairry oan is far from wyce.
There's nae respect. Ah try to gie advice,
But naw! There's that much argie-bargie it
's like nae place on earth but Paddy's Market.

DORINE.
If –

PERNELLE.
Can you no learn to shut your cheeky face?
You're jist a servin' lass, it's no your place
To stick your nose inty the business of your betters.

MARIANNE.
But, Gran! –

PERNELLE.
Wee Marianne. Obedient to the letter!

That auld-fashioned. So awfy-shy. Sae douce!
Butter widnae melt, she wouldny boo a goose.
Lukkin' oot thae big blue een and never blinkin' –
Ah bet your daddy's never shair whit you're thinkin'.

ELMIRE.
But . . . Mither –

PERNELLE.
                    Can you bring the wean up well
When you're scarce mair than a lassie yoursel'?
Her pair, deid, mither would turn in her grave
To see you spend, spend, spend what she scrimped to save.
A wummin needny get all dolled up sae fine
If it's only in her ain man's een she wants to shine.

CLÉANTE.
Come, now –

PERNELLE.
                    You're this bizzum's brother
Yet you and I have a lot of time for one another,
Am I right or am I wrang, eh, Mister Cléante?
You're . . . kinna half-sensible, yet I'd want –
If I were my son's wife – or him (which I'm no)
To ban you from this hearth, tell you to go.
How? Thae weys o'goin-oan, which you'd cry 'mense'.
Are mair leein' worldliness than honest commonsense.

CLÉANTE.
Orgon's Mister Tartuffe is a paragon, no doubt –

PERNELLE.
He is. See here, I take it ill-out
That you will scan him wi' that jaundiced eye!
Heed him. That man can not lie.

ELMIRE.
If we only did what Tartuffe saw fit
It'd be a gey grey life with damn-all fun in it.

DORINE.
Aye, hark at auld Narra-Mind and, afore lang,

We'd think ilka hermless thing we did was wrang.
Them that wants to can aye funn faut.

PERNELLE.

My son kens Tartuffe is worth his saut!
He'd raither you were in God's Good Grace
Than daunerin' doon your ain paths tae the Other Place.

MARIANNE.

Neither dad nor anybody can convince me
That he's sincere. I tell you, since he –
From the word go I couldn't stick one thing about him.
Valère says wan of these days he'll clout him!

PERNELLE.

And a' to sook in wi his future bride!
The big man! I'm shair Tartuffe is terrified!

DORINE.

Ah cry it a dampt disgrace
That a naebody should tak' the maister's place!
To breenge in here, a raggity bare-fit tink,
Wi' the bareface to tell us whit to think.

PERNELLE.

This humble hoose could be as a haly temple
If ye'd lukk–till his prayer, precept and example.

DORINE.

You think wan thing, Ah think anither.
You cry him a saint, Ah cry him a blether.

PERNELLE.

Oh the –

DORINE.

　　　　Him and his flunkie, Ah'd show them
Ah didny trust them further than Ah could throw them.

PERNELLE.

Aboot the sairvant, I neither care nor ken
But Tartuffe his maister is a Man Among Men
His truth's sairness and shairness is mair than you can thole,
Yet his yin thocht is your immortal soul.

DORINE.

> Hell's bells, if a neebor draps by fur tea
> Or Missis asks visitors in for a wee swaree,
> Where's the herm? What does he think'll happen
> That he nags us till our heids are nippin'?
> What kinnuffa bawdy-hoose does he think this is?
> Ah jalouse he's jealous of Missis.

PERNELLE.

> Haud yir wheesht, he's no the only yin
> To be annoyed by a' the gauns-oot-and-in
> And the caurs lined up wheel to wheel –
> Some o' Elmire's cronies, they areny real!
> Their sairvants are gallus, their gled-rags are garish –
> She micht mean nae herm, but she's the talk o' the pairrish.

CLÉANTE.

> Talk is cheap, and needs nae reason.
> For gossip, ach, it's aye the silly season
> And if we heed it, then we're dafter still.
> We could not stop the idle tongues that wish us ill
> Even if we shut our doors to our true friends.
> Ignore it! Our self respect depends
> On our clear consciences. Act fair and square,
> And what folk say is neither here nor there.

DORINE.

> Don't tell me! It's Daphne next door
> And that smouty wee man o' hers. They deplore
> Loud and lang, their clarty-minds imagine
> A'body but them's a bad yin.
> Ah say . . . it's them wi' guilty secrets o' their ain
> That are aye the first to cast the stane!
> 'Yon's a drunkert' 'She's a hure!' Sich brattle!
> It's a' a case o' the poat cryin' the kettle.

PERNELLE.

> Nuthin' to dae wi it! If you must know
> It was Orante who tellt me so!
> She's a guidly, godly soul and she
> Has plenty to say about your company.

This is exactly what DORINE *wants to know. Her face registers scorn.*

DORINE.
Well, nane can pick faut wi that guid wife!
Oh right enough she leads The Quiet Life –
At least since she got auld and past it!
She was wance so awfy-braw, but noo she's lost it .
She's very passremarkable 'boot ither folk!
The vera idea o' a cuddle gies her the boke
Yet, wance upon a time, she had mair men up her
Stairs and up her skirts than she had hoat suppers.
There's nae airn sae hard but rust'll fret it.
There's nae cloth sae fine but moths'll eat it.
So it shouldny surprise us when a soor auld biddy
Turns her back on the world that's turnt its back on her
                                        already.

During next speech DORINE, ELMIRE *and* MARIANNE
all mimic PERNELLE *behind her back as she wheels round
to almost but not quite catch each of them.* CLÉANTE *does
not join in but shakes his head and smiles on the three
women's complicity.* PERNELLE *catches him smiling at
this and wrongly accuses him of mocking her half way
through this next speech.*

PERNELLE (to ELMIRE).
These havers are what you wish was true!
(To DORINE.) I can't stand here all day listening to you
You neither ken nor care whit you're talking aboot
While yir fine mistress, day in, day oot
Mornin' noon and night wi a passion
Keeps this place gaun like a fair and fairs were gaun
                                        oot o' fashion!
But, if I can just get wan word in edgeweys tae mention
Somethin' that I fear you've yet to pey attention:
Till Tartuffe came you never knew that you were born
But my son never did yiz a better turn
Than to take inty his hame and heart this man
Who can convert you if anybody can.
He kens what's bad, he kens what's good and he
Kens what you should dae and what you shouldny.

Pairties and cerd-schools he canny abide
Because sich abominations are Auld Nick's pride.
And socials and swarrys and conversat-zionis
Will bring the wrath o' God doon oan us.
Oh, face to face it's kiss-ma-luif and palsy-walsy
But ahint your back you should hear whit they all say!
It's: 'That *will* be right' and 'I kennt it!'
And 'Yon yin's even blacker than he's pentit!'
Plenty reputations ruint, have nae doot!
Muck'll stick, when there's sae muckle fleein aboot.
And some folk are never happy till they're causin' trouble,
Yatterin' fit tae fill the vera tower o' Babel.
They'd frighten the French, and to cut a long story –
Ach well, Cleante, Sir, so you funn me a bore, eh?
Snirkle away then, and smirk up yir sleeve,
Ah've had mair than enough, it's time to leave!
Be a while afore I set fit again in this habitation,
Which has taken quite a tummle in my estimation.

Hits FLIPOTE.

Flipote! you're staunin'in a dwamm like a big daft dug!

PERNELLE.
Get a move oan or Ah'll gie you a skelp on the lug,
C'monty!

Exit PERNELLE, FLIPOTE, MARIANNE.

Scene Two

CLÉANTE *and* DORINE, *at ease together.*

CLÉANTE.
      I'll just stay here for now
In case, and for nothing, I get another row
From that old lady. She's beyond comprehension!

DORINE.
You're no feart! You ken better than mention

The words 'auld' and 'lady' in the wan braith.
She'd say: you're nae chicken either, you're baith
The wrang side o' forty, but speakin' for hersel'
She thinks she wears her years extremely well!

CLÉANTE.

No one said a word, she just hit the roof!
Incredible! She is quite besotted with Tartuffe.

DORINE.

You should see her son, if you think she's fond!
He is daft aboot the schunner, it's beyond
Rhyme, it's beyond reason or any sense at a'.
Orgon. Yince a man sae full o'commonsense an a'.
In oor Troubles he picked the winnin' side, served Mr. Prince
And loyally and bravely. But his heid's full o'mince
Noo that he's under Tartuffe's spell –
He loves him Not Wisely but Too Well.
He whispers in his ear and cries him brither.
Loves him mair than wife, dochter *or* mither.
Ah'll never unnerstaun whit compels him
To listen to Tartuffe and dae whit he tells him.
Och, as much o' a mystery to get to the erse y
As whit yin man sees in wan wummin, or vice versy.
In fact he treats Tartuffe – noo Ah come to mention–
No unlike a lassie he wis winchin' . . . .
Oh, it's aye the Place of Honour, the tap o' the table for
The man who eats mair than ony other six were able for.
It's, 'Noo, here's a tasty pick, dinna let the plate pass you.'
And gin Tartuffe should rift it's, 'My! God bless you.'

*Note of Molière's. A rare one, so it marks his own
astonishment at his character's boldness: 'It is a servant
who is speaking.'*

It makes me mad how everybody
Can see my maister is enamoured o' a *cuddy*.
Tartuffe canny brekk wind but it's a miracle.
Or open his mooth but it's an oracle.
Orgon bows doon to him in everything
Lowps lik' a puppet when Tartuffe pu's the string
Oh and peys through the nose for every sermon uttered

Because yon yin weel-kens whit side his breid is buttered
And hoo to herry money oot o' maister by a hunner ploys
Even his tyke o' a servin' man enjoys
The richt to harp and carp and criticise
Oor rouge and scent, which in *his* eyes–
Like lace and frills and a' thing the least fancy–
Are trappings o' devilishness and necromancy.
Nae sacrilege pit him in sic a tearing rage as
The hanky he funn in a hymnbook's pages!

Scene Three

Enter ELMIRE, *then* MARIANNE.

ELMIRE.
> Mither! She's said it all before once!
> Lucky you to miss the whole repeat performance.
> But here's my husband, I'm away before he sees me.
> Not one word, brother. Shsh! To please me.

Exit ELMIRE.

CLÉANTE.
> Suit yourself, sister. I'll stay
> If only to pass a civil time-of-day.

MARIANNE.
> Uncle, darlin', sound Dad out about my wedding.
> He refuses to discuss it. I bet it's Tartuffe spreading
> Rumours and mischief. We're happy, that sticks in his craw
> So he's been gettin'at Dad to make him hum and haw . . .
> Valère is mad about me and, needless to say,
> I just can't wait to name the day.
> And mibbe we –

DORINE *practically gags her, jumps in.*

DORINE.
> And here's the man himsel'.

Scene Four

Enter ORGON.

ORGON (*to* CLEANTE).
Hello, hello, how's it gaun? You're lookin' well.

MARIANNE*'s scurrying exit,* CLÉANTE *almost confused.*

CLÉANTE.
Its nice to see you. I'm just off.
How was the country? Green and stuff?

ORGON.
Haud on brother – Since Ah've been away, Dorine,
Tell me, the last twa-three days, how's everybody been?

To CLÉANTE.

See, yince hame Ah'm no' happy in masel'
Until Ah ken that a' the faimily's well.

DORINE.
Day afore yesterday Missis took a bad turn, the worst
O' high fevers, a heid thumpin' fit tae burst.

ORGON.
Och! An' Tartuffe?

DORINE.
                    Tartuffe! Oh fine. I think
You'll funn him fitter than fower fiddles, in the pink!

ORGON.
The sowell!

DORINE.
                    Come daurk, she wis richt weak
Wi' the gowpin' o' her sair heid and seeck
At the thocht o' touchin' a singel bite.

ORGON.
Och! An' Tartuffe?

DORINE.
>Oh, he sat down with appetite,
Demolished a gigot o' mutton and a brace
O' pairtridge right religiously afore her face.

ORGON.
The sowell!

DORINE.
>A' nicht she tossed and turned
And never got a wink, sae fierce her fever burned.

ORGON.
Och! An'Tartuffe?

DORINE.
>Riftin', dozent and weel-fed
He left the empty dishes, socht his bed
Whaur he slept a' nicht unfashed wi' guilt
Fartin' ablow the feather quilt.

ORGON.
The sowell!

DORINE.
>It lukked serious, we talked her,
Eventually, inty us sendin' fur the doctor.
Her temperature was skyhigh he sat up till the crisis –

ORGON.
Och. And Tartuffe?

DORINE.
>As large as life and twice as
Ugly! In spite o' Missus' fainting fit, he recovered fine!
And fortified himsel'wi fower jougs o' wine.

ORGON.
The sowell!

DORINE.
>They're *baith* better, Oh, your every
Concern, Ah'll tell Missus, wis for her recovery!

Exit DORINE.

Scene Five

CLÉANTE.

Brother! That bizzum's laughin'up her sleeve!
And – excuse me butting in – but I believe
She's got good reason. Why so blinkered?
You were good enough to take him in, now the dirty tinker'd
Take you to the cleaners! Charity by all means *but* –

ORGON.

You ken nothin' aboot nothin' so will you shut
That mooth o' yours, brither, afore Ah get upset?

CLÉANTE.

True, I don't know the man personally, and yet –
'By their *fruits* shall ye' – etcetera . . .

ORGON.

Brother, brother if you could getra
Chance to get to ken him, Ah ken you'd see –
He's a man who's . . . a richt . . . *Man* and he –
Och! To follow him is tae ken True Peace
To feel this midden o' a world release
Its haud upon ye. Chynged man, that's me!
Since Ah huv hud the benefit o' Tartuffe's company.
He says wordly ties are so much vanity.
And noo? Noo, wife, weans, mither could a' dee
And it wouldny cause me *that* much pain!

Snaps fingers.

CLÉANTE.

Oh that *is* nice, brother, real humane!

ORGON.

Och, if only you'd have been there
When Ah first encountert him and seen what Ah seen there.
He'd come each day to kirk wi' seemly modest mein,
His hale soul's fervour shinin' from his een –
Who wisnae inspired to see him kneelin' there,
Lips gaun nineteen-tae-the-dozen in silent prayer?

He Amen-ed and Hallelujah-ed and – the soul o' tact –
Humbly begged me to receive this holy tract
Which himsel' had funn sicc a boon and a blessing
He was moved to Spread the Word in passing.
Ah quizzed his servin'-man and he
Haltingly confessed his Maister's poverty. (*Shrugs*.)
Ah emptied my pockets, but, 'For goodness sake it
Is faur-faur too much' Tartuffe widnae take it!
Ah insistit. Oh, he canny lukkeftir his sel' at a',
Afore ma een, he gied the hauf o' it awa'!
(Oh they must've seen him comin'.)
Tae a' the cripples, cadgers and beggar-wummin!
For his ain protection Ah brocht him hame wi' me
Tae byde as yin o' the family.
Och, he's Luck Aboot the Hoose, Tartuffe!
Keeps a' thing richt ablow this roof.
He watches my wife's good name, Ah must say,
Ten-times mair jealously than Ah dae!
Mind you, he's ower hard upon his sel',
Yesterday the sowell wis right No Well,
Fair scourged wi' guilt because, wi richt-good relish
He'd cracked-deid a flea that bit him somethin' hellish!

CLÉANTE.

Where's your reason gone, I'm shocked!

ORGON.

Reason? Reason! God is not mocked!
Freethinkers, eh? Is that what they cry you?
I warn you: What's for you will not go by you.

CLÉANTE.

This is the usual from your kind.
You'd blindfold everybody else because you're blind.
He who sees clearly what is to be seen
Is a godless, freethinking libertine.
Spare me the sermons, God is my witness
And I'm not afraid to have him judge my moral fitness.
Piety, like bravery can be put on, – if we're as silly's
To believe in False Heroes and Holy Willies–
To fall for kidology and lose the place –

Not look for the true phizzog behind the falseface.
'The guinea-stamp is not the gold!'

ORGON.

Oh quite the philosoper! Well that's me told.
A solomon! A dominie! you're no' saft –
A peety that a' body but yirsel' is daft.

CLÉANTE.

Teacher nothing! Brother, I don't pretend
I'm clever – just, in the end,
It comes down to telling True from False.
Oh, nothing is more lovely than the quiet pulse
Of everyday piety in the true believer.
Nothing more sickening than the self deceiver –
The purveyor of platitudes that won't quite wash,
The sepulchre applying his own whitewash.
See, the ranting holyroller, born-again bigot, virgin birther
Member of the Elect, latterday crusader, fundamentalist
                                                  flat-earther
Is often as sincere as he is round the bend!
Much worse, the blatant charlatan! For his own ends,
He cynically exploits what mankind most reveres,
Manipulates our deepest, most sacred, hopes and fears.
These days it's not at all uncommon
To hear fat, rich, priests decrying mammon.
Pastmasters all at twisting the text
So they profit in this world by way of the next.
They trade in pie-in-the-sky and (can you beat it?)
Here in this world they have their cake and cat it.
Doubly dangerous, these demons, whose best weapon
Is our reverence. We give them power to step on
Everyone and everything, and all in God's Name!
They are quick to anger, quicker still to blame.
They call down Heaven's Wrath to help them do their worst
Before they stick in the knife and twist, they bless it first.
These days such villains are all around.
But altruism and true piety can still be found!
There are those who, quite without vanity,
Embody Faith and Hope and Charity.
You know such men. They don't show off

Yet their humane example is enough
To inspire us lesser men to emulate.
Arrogant preachiness is what they hate.
They are not always sniffing out intrigue; they find
Politicking absurd; they have no axe to grind.
They see the good in everyone and have the inner
Strength to hate the sin, yet love the sinner.
This is indeed the way to live!
Frankly, your man Tartuffe, forgive
Me, is not any kind of good example.
You act in good faith, but the explanation's simple.
A case of all that glitters and so on . . .

ORGON.

Are you feenished, brother? Do go on!

CLÉANTE.

Enough said!

ORGON.

                Thank God for that, excuse me . . .

CLÉANTE.

One word! Let's change the subject, don't refuse me.

ORGON.

Uh-huh?

CLÉANTE.

          A wee bird told me a certain young man
By the name of Valère was to wed Marianne?

ORGON.

Uh-huh

CLÉANTE.

          And that you had fixed the happy day?

ORGON.

Uh-huh.

CLÉANTE.

          Why than defer the ceremony?

ORGON.

Ah dinny ken.

CLÉANTE.

But you've had second thoughts, or third?

ORGON.
Mibbe.

CLÉANTE.
You mean then to go back upon your word?

ORGON.
Ah didny say that . . .

CLÉANTE.

Surely no just impediment
To make a man break a promise he said he meant?

ORGON.
Mibbe aye, mibbe hooch-aye.

CLÉANTE.

Don't beat about
The bush, what are you so suddenly discreet about?
Actually, Valère himself asked me to ask you.

ORGON.
For heaven's sake!

CLÉANTE.

– A task you
Are making very hard. What'll I tell the boy?

ORGON.
Whatever you like.

CLÉANTE.
Shall I say no joy?
What are your plans, sir?

ORGON.

I plan
To let heaven guide me.

CLÉANTE.

Come on man!
You made Valère a promise then, it seems, forgot
It. Will you keep your word or not?

ORGON.
  Tattibye!

CLÉANTE.
      Poor Valère! Altogether
  It looks like I better warn him. Stormy weather!

  End of Act One.

ACT TWO

Scene One

ORGON *enters and starts looking in cupboards.*

ORGON.
  Marianne!

MARIANNE.
            Daddy! (*She enters.*)

ORGON.
                  C'mere to me
  I want a quiet word.

MARIANNE.
                  What are you looking for?

ORGON.
                              To see
  If anybody is hidin' tryin' to overhear.
  This wee press is just the place for sich a nosy ear!
  Naw, naw we're okey-dokey. Hmmm. Marianne, hen,
  You're sicc an awfy nice-natured lass ye ken,
  And you've aye kept yir auld daddy company

MARIANNE.
  You've been the best daddy in the world to me.

ORGON.
  That's nice. If your wish to please me is heartfelt
  You'll want to dae exactly whit you're tellt.

MARIANNE.
  To please ma daddy is to please masel'

ORGON.
  Hoo do ye feel about Tartuffe? Think well!

MARIANNE.
Who me?

ORGON.
Aye you. Take yir time, but Ah haveny got a' day.

MARIANNE.
Aw naw! Aw aye . . . Whit do you want me to say?

ORGON.
Sensible question yon! Well, tell me, Marianne,
That our guest's a fine upstaunin' man,
You're awfy fond o' him, naebody ye'd raither
Mairry than Tartuffe, an' please yir faither,
Whit?

MARIANNE.
Whit!

ORGON.
Whit's up?

MARIANNE.
Whit did ye say?

ORGON.
Whit?

MARIANNE.
Some mistake?

ORGON.
How?

MARIANNE.
Who's the man that I'm supposed to take?
Who am I so awfy fond o' there's naebody I'd raither
Marry? Shairly I didny hear you, faither?

ORGON.
Tartuffe.

MARIANNE.
But I do nothing of the kind, so why
Would ma ain faither wish me to lie?

ORGON.

>Because Ah want fur it to be true
>And whit Ah want should be enough for you.

MARIANNE.

>Daddy, you widnae –

During next ORGON *tiptoes up to door and flings it open.*

ORGON.

>   Would Ah no!
>Tartuffe and you will mairry, so!
>That's that! A family alliance, got that clear?
>My mind's made up.

>DORINE, *bent over at keyhole, falls into room.*

Scene Two

ORGON.

>   Whit urr *you* daein' here?
>Nosy bitch to spy on us like that.
>D'you no hear 'bout curiosity an' the cat?

DORINE.

>It must be just a kid-oan, shairly?
>Must huv the wrang end o' the stick, yet Ah'm fairly
>Positive Ah heard somethin' 'boot a marriage in the offin'
>That vernear had me die o' laughin'!

ORGON.

>Is it sae unbelievable?

DORINE.

>   Oh aye,
>And Ah don't believe you don't know why!

ORGON.

>Ah ken whit'll make you believe it.

DORINE.

Tell us a wee jackanory, we're a' ears to receive it!

ORGON.

Ah'll tell you, and soon you'll see it come to pass.

MARIANNE.

Oh naw!

ORGON.

Oh aye, nae kiddin' lass!

DORINE.

Och, didnae pey ony attention tae yir paw.
It's jist a huntigowk!

ORGON.

Ah tell you – !

DORINE.

Nut at a',

Naebody'll swally this!

ORGON.

Ah'm startin' tae get mad!

DORINE.

A'right, keep yir hair oan, but it's sad
Hoo a man mair than auld enough tae be wise,
Who sports grey hairs on whiskers o' sicc size,
Could be daft enough to think he'd want –

ORGON.

The nerve!

You tak' a lot mair liberties than you deserve
To get away wi'. Shut yir face!

DORINE.

A'right, a'right, don't lose the place.
Let's discuss this quietly and keep calm . . .
Ah canny tell you how amazed Ah am.
What would yon bigot want wi'oor wee lassie?
He's plenty else to keep him busy!
An who's he onywey, when he's at hame?

How, wi' a' your money *and* your name
You'd want a gaberlunzie son-in-law . . . ?

ORGON.

Enough!
We should lukk up to him who lukks doon on such stuff
As getting and spendin', a' the world's gowd and gear.
He's been ower concerned wi heaven to prosper here!
Mibbe Ah cin restore his fortunes and fill his pantry –
Back whaur he comes fae, ken, he's yin o' the gentry!

DORINE.

Gentry! Heard it, heard it! – Fair enough, unless
The famous holiness disnae go wi' snobbishness?
Och Ah see Ah vex you, but why sich swank?
A'right! Stick to the man himsel', forget the rank.
Think aboot it! To gie wee Marianne,
Sae young and bonny, to sicc an auld man!
Imagine the consequences it'd bring.
Whit'd happen wid be the Usual Thing!
To live the virtuous life is awfy chancy
When a lassie's merrit tae a man she disnae fancy.
And the man who kens the finger-o-scorn's
Pinted at him because he weers the horns
Has *made* his wife nae better than she should be!
Pure? Merrit tae the richt man she could be
So the man who gie's his dochter's haun should ken that it's
Him that's responsible for the sins she commits.
Think! Afore you get her in sich slaister!

ORGON.

Oh! The servin-lass gie's her orders tae the maister!

DORINE.

Who could dae a lot worse than dae whit she'd tell him!

ORGON.

Marianne! Don't listen tae this dampt haiverin'bellum.
Trust your daddy, he kens whit's guid for ye!
Ah ken, young Valère had made a bid for ye –
But Ah've since heard he gambles, is a bit o' a drinker
And, Ah suspeck, an atheistical free thinker –
Ah don't see him at the kirk, he disnae go.

DORINE.

Should he go at certain times and all for show?

ORGON.

When Ah want your opinion, miss, Ah'll ask!
Marianne, Tartuffe and his guidwife'll bask
In Heaven's ilka blessing, and sich treasure
Will merely crown their earthly pleasure!
Like weans in the wid, like twa turtledoos
Like a richt perra lovebirds, like coos
Rolling in clover, like moths tae the light
They'll attract yin anither, happy as pigs in – right
Piggy-paradise, that's the pure and simple y it!
An' – a clever lass can aye mak' a man tae fit her template.

DORINE.

She canny mak' a silk purse oot a soo's erse!

ORGON.

The language!

DORINE.

                    An eejit is an eejit, nothin' worse!
Yon yin husnae got the sense he wis born wi!
Plenty bumps on his heid, but, tae grow horn wi!

ORGON.

Dinna interrupt! Cin you no learn
No tae stick yir nose inty whit's nane o' yir concern?

Turns to speak to MARIANNE, *but each time* DORINE
interrupts him as soon as he goes to open his mouth.

DORINE.

Ah wid say nuthin' if Ah didny care aboot ye!

ORGON.

That's awfy guid o'ye. Ah could dae withoot ye . . .

DORINE.

And 'cos Ah care –

ORGON.

                    Who cares if you care or no!

DORINE.

But Ah'll care'boot you onywey, Ah will so!

ORGON.

Ocht! Will you shut up?

DORINE.

Ah cry it a sin
Yon's the sort o' alliance ye want yir dochter in.

ORGON.

You brassnecked neb you, ya bletheranskite –

DORINE.

Whit! Is this the big religious man, dae Ah hear right?

ORGON.

A saint'd lose patience, you should be hung!
For the last time, Ah mean it! Haud yir tongue.

DORINE.

If Ah don't speak oot, Ah'll think it a' the mair.

ORGON.

Think whit you like, but open yir mooth, beware!

To MARIANNE.

Ah've thocht o' everythin' –

DORINE (aside)

Ah'm fair beelin'
At no bein' able to say whit Ah'm feelin'.

But as ORGON *turns to her she always shuts up. He always turns back then to* MARIANNE.

ORGON.

Tartuffe isny o' yir dandified or cissy ilk
And yet his face is . . .

DORINE.

Fit tae turn the milk!

ORGON.

. . . Is such that, even if you don't care
For his other qualities –

DORINE.

> They'll make A Lovely Pair!
>
> If Ah wiz her, nae man'd mairry me,
> No if Ah didny want him! He'd soon see,
> And see afore the weddin' day was by,
> Ye can tak' a wife tae bed but ye canny mak' her lie.

ORGON.

You mean tae tak' nae heed o' whit Ah say?

DORINE.

Whit's up? It isny you Ah'm talkin' tae.

ORGON.

Who were ye talkin' tae, then?

DORINE.

> Masel'.

ORGON.

A'richt. Naebody cin say Ah didny warn her well!
Ah'm forced to gie her the back o' ma haun . . .

To MARIANNE, *tempting and daring* DORINE.

Ah ken ye'll be happy, learn tae unnerstaun –
The man Ah've picked – The future Ah've mapped oot

> so well.

(*Bursts.*) How are you no talkin' tae yirsel?

DORINE.

Ah've naethin' tae say.

ORGON.

> Jist wan word –

DORINE.

Ah talk when it suits me.

ORGON.

> Cheep awa', wee burd!

DORINE.

Ah'm no sae daft.

ORGON.

                    A'richt, Marianne,
    You've tae dae everythin' Ah tell ye an' mairry this man.

DORINE (bursts out then runs away, dodging blow).
    Ah'd be daft enough tae mairry him an' Ah don't think!

He takes a swipe, but misses of course.

ORGON.
    That maid o' yours wad drive me tae drink.
    Ah'm no fit to continue the conversation thanks to yon.
    Ma bloodpressure's up an ma insides are gaun!
    Ah better funn ma medicine an' dose masel'.
    Tak' a turn aboot the gairden an' compose masel'.

    Exit ORGON *leaving* MARIANNE *and* DORINE.

Scene Three

DORINE.
    Huz the cat got your tongue, or whit?
    Leavin' me tae say your bit!
    The hale thing's ridic-ulous, nae sense t'it
    But naw, ye nivir said a word against it.

MARIANNE.
    Ma faither's the Big Boss, let's drop it –

DORINE.
    Say onythin', dae onythin', but stop it.

MARIANNE.
    Say what?

DORINE.
                    Tell him ye canny boss the hert aboot.
    Say love is the wan thing ye'll no mairry withoot.
    Say if he's so ta'en oan wi Tartuffe, oh well
    Mibbe he should mairry him himsel'.

MARIANNE.

His power over me's as absolute as it's absurd!
And I'm feart tae say a single word.

DORINE.

C'moan! Valère 's already asked ye, so
Tell me, d'you love him, eh, or d'you no?

MARIANNE.

Oh Dorine, that isny fair!
How can you ask! You know how much I care.
Day and night you've been my confidante
You know Valère 's the only man I'll ever want.

DORINE.

How dae Ah ken a' that heart-tae-heart
Wisnae jist talk, and playin' the part?

MARIANNE.

Dorine, I can't tell you how hurt I feel
If even you can doubt my love is real.

DORINE.

Then you love him?

MARIANNE.

More than my life.

DORINE.

And he loves you?

MARIANNE.

Enough to make his wife.

DORINE.

Fine. And how aboot the big Tartuffe Marriage Plan?

MARIANNE.

I'll kill myself before I'm forced to marry such a man.

DORINE.

Oh very good! Ah must be daft to no see
The easy wey oot o' a' this hertbrek is tae dee!
Is yon no awfy sensible, the very dab!
My! self peety fair gies ye the gift o' the gab.

MARIANNE.

You're that crabbit, you're no offering
Much help or pity for me in my suffering.

DORINE.

Nae peety for them that cause a big stramash and yit
Jist gie in when it comes tae the bit.

MARIANNE.

I'm feart to just say I'll no wed him!

DORINE.

Love asks you hae a lover's smeddum!

MARIANNE.

It's no a question of how much I love Valère.
He should deal wi dad for me, so there!

DORINE.

Guid kens yir da's deleerit ower yon!
But whit Valère's done wrang, Ah fail tae unnerstaun.
Because he took Orgon at his word but noo discovers
Yir dad's gone back on it, the faut's your lover's?

MARIANNE.

Am I supposed to be stubborn and defiant
Pit my wee self against my dad, the giant?
Is it no kinna unfeminine to flaunt
Before the whole wide world how much I want
Valère? Should a lassie disobey her faither?

DORINE.

Of course she shouldny, no when she'd raither
Have yit another auld man to belang tae!
Tartuffe! That's grand! 'Deed Ah'd be wrang tae
Try and pit yi aff, faur be it fae me!
Jined wi Mister Tartuffe in Holy Matrimony!
That's no tae be sniffed at, he's – so the world's heard –
The Big Aristocrat – in his ain back-yerd.
Wi' his rid, plooky grunzie – is he no quite it!
If you're pleased hen, I'm delightit.

MARIANNE.

Aw naw!

DORINE.

     Oh aye, ye'll be mistress o' sich cherms
When ye lie a' nicht in yir bridegroom's erms . . .

MARIANNE.

 Don't! Ah canny. Tell me whit tae dae.

DORINE.

 Naw naw, A biddable good-lassie must obey
 Her faither if he'd wad her tae a puggy-ape!
 Yir future's rosy, dinna ettle tae escape.
 He'll tak' ye till his ain neck o' the wids
 Introduce ye tae his clan o' cousins, bluid's
 Thicker than watter, they'll be yir sole society.
 – Bar the cooncillor's wife who, wi' propriety
 Will tak' you ben the parlour, dust the chair
 Afore she says 'Noo park your erse doon there'.
 Mibbe yince a year there'll be a galaday
 Wi' twa sets o' bagpipes an' a flag fur the holiday!
 And if your man –

MARIANNE.

     Over my dead body, Dorine!
 Tell me how to get out of it, don't be mean.

DORINE.

 Ah'm jist the servant –

MARIANNE.

     Oh in the name!

DORINE.

 Yi deserve tae go through wi' it a' the same.

MARIANNE.

 Dorine, pet!

DORINE.

   Naw.

MARIANNE.

    I swear to you, I'll die!

DORINE.

 Naw, Tartuffe's the bed yiv made, and ye maun lie.

MARIANNE.

Help me, I've always trusted you, I've aye relied –

DORINE.

Naw, it serves ye richt if yir Tartuffified!

MARIANNE.

Very well. I suffer. You don't care
So leave me now, alone with my despair. –
Despair which shall teach my misery
The One, Unfailing, Final Remedy . . .

Turns to go, DORINE *stops her.*

DORINE.

Haud oan, it seems yi need Auld Dorine's help at last
In spite o' a' yir dampt cheek in the past?

MARIANNE.

Abandon me to this Living Hell, you
Abandon me to Death. I'll die, I tell you!

DORINE.

There, there, we'll fox them, be ower clever
For the likes o' them. Well, here's the lover!

Scene Four

Enter VALÈRE.

VALÈRE.

Aha! Exactly who I'd choose to see –
I just heard some news that certainly was news to me.

MARIANNE.

What?

VALÈRE.

That you are marrying Tartuffe.

MARIANNE.

It's true
My father seems to have this end in view.

VALÈRE.

Your father, miss, –

MARIANNE.

Decided I'm at his disposal
Reversed our plans and made a new proposal.

VALÈRE.

What! In seriousness?

MARIANNE.

In seriousness
He tells me my only answer can be yes.

VALÈRE.

And did you tell him where to go?

MARIANNE.

What do you think I told him?

VALÈRE.

I don't know!

MARIANNE.

Well if you don't know, I don't either!

VALÈRE.

You don't?

MARIANNE.

I don't.

VALÈRE.

That's honest! Suppose it's neither
Here nor there as far as I'm concerned . . .

MARIANNE.

It's what?

VALÈRE.

No skin off my nose quite honestly, it's not!

MARIANNE.
It's not?

VALÈRE.
                Not really

MARIANNE.
                No? That's nice.
All the same I'd be awfully glad of your advice.
Should I marry him or not?

VALÈRE.
                            Of course!
Marry the man, you could certainly do worse.

MARIANNE.
You're right, I'll do it! Thanks for the Balanced View.

VALÈRE.
Evidently this prospect is agreeable to you.

MARIANNE.
As agreeable as your role of Agony Aunt?

DORINE (aside).
A quarrel is a hellish whirlpool lovers want.
They must! They *will* wade in an' hit oot blindly.

MARIANNE (*to* VALÈRE).
Thank you for your counsel, I know you meant it kindly.

VALÈRE.
A pleasure, madam, to give you the answer you desired.

MARIANNE.
You wish me to marry him, sir, I'll do what's required.

DORINE (*to herself*).
Leave them, Dorine, tae their fechts and fankles . . .

Withdraws and looks on with amusement.

VALÈRE.
You never loved me, that's what rankles.
Boy! When I think how easily I was deceived!

MARIANNE.

Huh! And the advice that I received!
Don't talk to me of 'never loved', excuse me!
I'll marry who you advised me to, since you refuse me.

VALÈRE.

Advice nothing! Excuse enough
To spurn my love and break it off.

MARIANNE.

That will be right!

VALÈRE.

Of course it is
You're over the moon you're going to be his.

MARIANNE.

Think what you want to think, I don't mind.

VALÈRE.

I will. And mibbe I'll pay you back in kind.
I know another lady and I'm Well In there . . .

MARIANNE.

Sure, not a female in the world but fancies Valère!

VALÈRE.

Obviously not true, since *you* don't.
But *someone* might, if you won't.
I'm sure some sweet, kind lady can be found
To dish out consolation on the rebound!

MARIANNE.

The gap I leave is not so big you won't fill it.
Be real easy to find someone better, will it?

VALÈRE.

I'll do my best. Hell, it's self-defence!
Losing you has wrecked my confidence.
But, if the wounds of love are far from healed,
Still, in like Flynn and play the field,
Lay on Macduff – rather than be humiliated
Being seen to love where it's not appreciated.

MARIANNE.

How noble! How too, too masculine!

VALÈRE.

Anyone following these principles is doing fine.
I've to keep my flame of love for you a white hot anguish?
You'd want me to be lovelorn? I've to languish
While visions of you and him dance in my head
And not put my love elsewhere instead?

MARIANNE.

On the contrary, find some slut then! Do your stuff.
Far as I'm concerned yesterday's not soon enough.

VALÈRE.

I'm sure you're happy all this has resulted
In my leaving you for ever, totally insulted?

He goes to leave, but keeps returning, again and again.

MARIANNE.

Too true!

VALÈRE.

      I want you to remember thanks to you, alas,
Matters between us have come to total impasse.

MARIANNE.

Uh-huh!

VALÈRE.

      My plan is very simple.
You marry? I'll follow your example.

MARIANNE.

So be it.

VALÈRE.

      So be it indeed, okey-dokey, right-oh!

MARIANNE.

Fine!

VALÈRE.

      Last time you'll see me, I want you to know.

MARIANNE.
 I'll survive.

VALÈRE.
     Eh?

MARIANNE.
     Eh what?

VALÈRE.
       Did you shout?

MARIANNE.
 Me, you're dreaming!

VALÈRE.
      I'm on my way out
 You hear me? Goodbye!

MARIANNE.
      Goodbye, good riddance!

DORINE.
 Hoi, Ah nivir heard sich bliddy nonsense.
 You're a daft pair o' articles, ah don't know!
 Ah let ye fight, tae see hoo faur ye'd go.
 Hoi! Stoap Valère.

VALÈRE.
    What's up, Dorine?

DORINE.
 C'mere!

VALÈRE.
   No, I'm adamant, I mean
 To leave once and for all, at *her* suggestion!

DORINE.
 Stoap!

VALÈRE.
   I can't. It's quite out of the question.

MARIANNE.
 Evidently he can't stand to see my face!
 I'll go and leave him plenty empty space.

MARIANNE *goes to leave.* DORINE *lets go of* VALÈRE *and grabs her.*

DORINE.
Another yin! Where ye gaun?

MARIANNE.

                              Leave me!

DORINE.

                                        Haud oan!

MARIANNE.
No! No, Dorine I'm off, leave me alone.

VALÈRE.
I'll be the one to go, I feel compelled.
Marianne looks at me as though I smelled.

DORINE *grabs him still hanging on to* MARIANNE.

DORINE.
Again! Yiz'll be the daith o'me!
Don't be stupit! C'mere the baith o' ye.

MARIANNE.
Dorine, what do you want with us?

VALÈRE.
I fear we've nothing further to discuss.

DORINE.
Ah'm gonny sort this fankle oot, cause some'dy needs
Tae! Are ye baith aff yir heids?

VALÈRE.
She said a lot of things I can't forget.

DORINE.
Urr ye an eejit or urr ye an eejit tae get upset?

MARIANNE.
I was treated in a very pretty fashion!

DORINE.
Daft as each other! Her yin passion
Is you and yours, I swear!

And this boay couldny love you mair.
He's fairly burnin' tae be yir man.
C'moan Valère! Acht! Marianne . . .

MARIANNE.
Why then give me such advice?

VALÈRE.
Why ask me? That wasn't very nice.

DORINE.
A perra loonies! Gie's yir haun's, you twa.
(*To* VALÈRE.) Yours first!

VALÈRE.
                                          What for?

DORINE (*taking* MARIANNE'*s and linking them*).
                                          Yours an' a'!

MARIANNE.
What exactly is the point of this?

DORINE.
Guid's sake, gi'e yin anither a Wee Kiss.
Sic a remedy wid be entirely . . . efficacious.

VALÈRE (*to* MARIANNE).
Give me a civil look then, don't be ungracious!

DORINE.
De'il kens, but lovers are gey thrawn craturs . . .

VALÈRE.
No wonder men end up as women-haters.
After all those cruel, cruel things you've spoken –
It's not just Valère's poor *heart* you've broken!

MARIANNE.
You're a most ungrateful man! That's great!

DORINE.
Enough o' a' this argie-bargie and debate –
Hoo can we pit a stoap tae this accursit mairrage?

MARIANNE.
Let's stop it, please! Valère, screw your courage!

Once he's worked out this isn't an insult he grabs her and
they kiss. They kiss and stop and kiss again all through
DORINE's *next (practical) speech so she's constantly*
exasperated that they're taking nothing in.

DORINE.
If yir dad's conscience disnae prick him,
Then, somehow, we'll funn a wey to swick him.
Let oan yir fu' fae tap to toe wi' dochterly devotion
An' that ye 'gree till the hale jingbang o' a notion.
Then, when it comes tae the bit, the weddin'
Can aye be pit aff at a fiddler's biddin'.
Yin time, yir no weel – a sair heid, or worse;
Anither ye broke a mirror; or met a hearse
As ye were on yer wey tae kirk; you're in a guddle
Ower a bad dream 'boot mucky watter in a puddle
Or . . . ye seen a single pyat, a burd o' sicc ill omen
The day's nae day tae mak'ye a mairrit wummin.
An' here's yir trump-cerd, unless ye say 'I do',
Nae man oan earth can be yokit tae you.
Hooever, in oarder tae best speed our thrivance,
You two ignore each other, that's oor furst contrivance!

DORINE *prises them apart, and to* VALÈRE.

DORINE.
Get tae! Enlist yir freens in a campaign
To mak' her faither gie whit's, eftir a', yir ain!
As for us, we've a'ready the stepmither
On oor side, next: that Man o' Pairts, her brither.

VALÈRE.
Whatever is the end of all our machinations
In you, my darling, lie my dearest aspirations.

MARIANNE.
If my cruel father should insist on tearing us apart
Still no man but Valère shall ever rule my heart.

DORINE.
Would lovers no deive you, their mooth's don't stap!
I said, get tae!

VALÈRE.

        Another thing –

DORINE.

              Yap,yap,yap!
Yir tongue's gaun like the clappers, ye blether.
You go wan wey – and *you* go the ither!

Separates them and shoves them off, one each side, stands arms akimbo, breathing.

End of Act Two

ACT THREE

Scene One

DORINE*'s respite shattered as first* VALÈRE, *then a moment later* MARIANNE, *from their respective sides reappear.*

VALÈRE.

    May God strike me dead – No don't call me rash,
    I mean it. Tartuffe! I'll settle his hash,
    I'll – I don't deserve to be called a man
    If any power in the world keep me from Marianne.

    The lovers rush into each other's arms.

DORINE.

    Oh aye, 'Haud ma jaicket!' –'Haud yir hoarses,
    Orgon mibbe isny serious, of course he's
    Likely no! Onywey, fechtin', whaur's the sense in that?
    A loat mair weys than yin tae skin a cat . . .

MARIANNE.

    Oh don't do it Valère! D'you think I'd enjoy to see
    Two grown men fighting, and all over me?
    Forget Tartuffe! I'd never marry him anyway.
    Dorine'll tell you I refused point blank. No way!

DORINE.

    But yir steptmither! Gently does it baith o' ye –
    She'll soart Tartuffe, and yir faither tae!
    Tartuffe's aye sookin' in wi her and it's ma theory
    He's got an awfy soft spot fur Elmire. Eh?
    You've never noticed? Mibbe Ah read too much intae
    The slaiverin' pee-hereness that you're blin' tae
    At ony rate: Missis somehow discovered
    Orgon's daft scheme and how yir lover'd
    Jist get the bum's rush, wi' nae by-yir-leave,
    So ye'd mairry Tartuffe – well she couldnae believe

It! How could it come up Orgon's humph
To abandon his dochter tae yon big sumph?
As for yir wee pow-wow, she wis jist remarkin'
How she'd gie her eye-teeth t' be able tae hearken
(Flee-on-the-wa' style) tae you an' yir pop . . .
Ah says, 'Ah'll funn a hidey-hole . . .' She goes, 'Eavesdrop?'
Ah goes 'Aye', she goes, 'Naw! I couldny encourage it.'
Ah goes, 'Suit yirsel', well!' She says, 'Could you manage it?'
Well: nothin' fur it, tae cut a longstory shoart,
But fur me tae hide, hearken and report –
Back tae Elmire, like – whether it was true.
So! Ah've an eye tae the keyhole keekin' through
Takin'a' thing in, when whit should happen
But Orgon catches us! Rid-haundit, ears flappin'!
Nae maitter! Afore a' this, Elmire
Asked me tae ask Tartuffe tae meet her here,
Aye, *she'll* sound him oot aboot this mairage –
She's on *your* side, she'll saut his purridge
Guid an' proper if he entertains the notion
Sicc a' pairrin' widna cause a right commotion.
Onywey, she'll fyke oot how he feels aboot it
And convince the galoot; better dae withoot it!
Well, when ah went tae arrange this wee rendezvous
Tartuffe's servin' man gie'd me quite a talkin'-to
For ettlin' tae disturb Maister ett his Evenin' Prayers.
– However, ony meenit noo, he'll be doon the stairs
And if you two skedaddle, noo dinnae ask why!
Ah'll nab Tartuffe as he goes by.

VALÈRE.

I'll stay right here and grab the devil.

DORINE.

Naw, leave it tae me –

VALÈRE.

      I'll be civil!

DORINE.

Civil nothing, you'll lose the heid
And that, young lovers, would be a' we need!
Get!

MARIANNE.
Valère's right! He'll be diplomatic.

DORINE.
Here he 's! Hide! Is this no pathetic?

Scurrying about, DORINE *finally gets* VALÈRE *into one cupboard,* MARIANNE *into another.*

Scene Two

Enter TARTUFFE *followed by his man,* LAURENT. *Perceiving an audience in* DORINE *he acts up to it.*

TARTUFFE.
Laurent! Awa' an' lock up ma King James Bible.
An' bring me linament – Ah'm awfy liable
Tae rheumaticks wi' bein' so lang oan the caul' flair, kneelin'
It sterts wi peens an' needles then Ah lose a' feelin' . . .
It's gi'ein' me gyp, so git thon embrocation – Och an' pit
ma bookmerk in whaur Ah wis readin': *Lamentations!*

. . . The Lord hath accomplished his fury . . . they that were brought up in scarlet shall embrace dunghills . . . '

DORINE (aside).
'Laurent! Knot ma scourge again, mak' shair it hurt.
An' hem an extra awfy jaggy bit on ma hairshirt.'
Whit a big ham! He must think Ah'm green.
(*Aloud.*) Excuse me!

TARTUFFE (*aside*).
                    Well, yon's a sich fur richt sair een!
(*Aloud.*) Ach, *chist* a minute there, Ah'll thank yi
Afore ye speak tae me tae tak' this hanky
In the name o' a' that's holy and religious –

DORINE.
Whit fur?

TARTUFFE.

> To cover up yir . . . yir . . . whidjies.
It's evil sichts lik' yon, I'm sure it is.
That swall men's thochts wi' impurities.

DORINE.

You must be awfy fashed wi' flesh tae fire
Yir appetites sae quick wi' Base Desire.
As fur masel', Ah'm no that easy steered.
If you were barescud-nakit, aye and geared
Up guid and proaper, staunin'hoat for houghmagandie
I could lukk and lukk at you, and no get randy.

TARTUFFE.

You should wash oot that mooth wi soap!
Ah'm going. You'll repent, I hope.

DORINE.

No, *Ah'm* away, but first of all:
My mistress asked me to ask you could she pay a call?
– With all respect, sir, it'   s a maitter of some delicacy . . .
Would you kindly grant her an audience just now, in

> privacy . . .

TARTUFFE.

Oh but maist certainly!

DORINE (*aside*).

> As nice as pie!
Ah think Ah was right the furst time, aye . . .

TARTUFFE.

Will she be long?

DORINE.

Doon these stairs will come, wha else,
Elmire. I'll lea' yiz by yir ain twa sel's.

Exit DORINE *pantomiming as much as possible to the
entering* ELMIRE.

Scene Three

TARTUFFE.
> May merciful heaven grant to thee and thine
> Health, wealth and grace baith temporal and divine.
> I, God's humblest servant ask, and ask in all sincerity,
> May He crown you all your days wi' bountiful prosperity.

ELMIRE.
> I'm much obliged, you're far too kind, now please
> Let's sit down and be a wee bit more at ease . . .

TARTUFFE.
> Ah trust you are nae longer . . indisposed?

ELMIRE.
> I'm fine. It was jist a wee virus, I suppose.

TARTUFFE.
> God's guid indeed, that he should grant
> Tae me, a miserable sinner a' Ah want –
> For ma every desire in prayer and supplication
> Was for your Guild Health and Total Restoration.

ELMIRE.
> Thank you, but such concern's, I'm sure, excessive –

TARTUFFE.
> Noo that's impossible, in earnestness Ah've
> Begged the Lord tae spare your health and tak' ma ain.

ELMIRE.
> I'm sure such useless sacrifice were no one's gain –
> I'm very grateful, though, to you . . .

TARTUFFE.
> Sich loving-kindness is only what you're due.

ELMIRE.
> There's a certain wee something – Can I bend your ear?
> It's . . . fortunate we're so private and secluded here . . .

TARTUFFE.

Alane wi' you at last – I'm quite delightit.

And very gled oor pleasure's mutual and requitit!

Ah've often intercedit wi' the Lord fur sich a circumstance

But heaven, till noo, 's denied tae me the chance.

ELMIRE.

– Speaking as (to all intents and purposes) Marianne's

mother . . .

Mr. Tartuffe, can we be . . . open and unbuttoned with each

other?

TARTUFFE.

My dearest wish, Mistress, is to lay bare

My hert and soul – incidentally, I swear

What you micht, erronously, have thocht was me criticizin'

The company you keep – actually this lies in

A zeal for *you*, in case you're misinterpreted.

Were they to cry you 'scarlet wummin' I'd see red!

In fact I'd –

ELMIRE.

It's easy to tell fair

From false, and know who's for your welfare –

He presses the ends of her fingers.

TARTUFFE.

Right you are, pre-zactly, and needless to say –

ELMIRE.

Ooyah, you're nipping!

TARTUFFE.

I got carried away!

Ah'd dee raither than hurt you, Ah care faur

Too much to ever –

His hand has dropped to her knee.

ELMIRE.

What's your hand down there for?

TARTUFFE.

An *awfy* bonny frock, it mak's you every inch a lady

Ah wiz fair . . . ta'en up wi' seein' whit it's made y!
Ah canny tell felt fae velveteen you see!

ELMIRE *removes hand deftly.*

ELMIRE.
The *dress* is velvet, the only thing that's felt's ma knee.

Molière's direction: she pushes back her chair and
TARTUFFE *draws his nearer.*

TARTUFFE (*gawping down* ELMIRE*'s cleavage and fingering
     the lace at the neckline*).
Goodness gracious, when you lukk intae it
The lacey-work they're daein nooadays is awfy intricate!
I can't imagine onythin' pit together better.

ELMIRE.
Right enough, but about this Other Metter . . .
They say my husband's going to break his word and you
And my stepdaughter are to marry . . . Is this true?

In unison, behind them, fixed on ELMIRE *and* TARTUFFE,
VALÈRE *slowly sticks his head out and* MARIANNE,
listening.

TARTUFFE.
Wee skliff o' a lassie – och he did mention
The ghost o' the idea, but Ah've nae intention –
Confidentially, elsewhere than in a mairriage wi' a wean
Lies the Blissful Ecstacy I hope I micht attain.

ELMIRE.
That's because your minds on Higher Things, you're not
As Other Men –

TARTUFFE.
                    – Ma hert's no made of stone ye ken –

ELMIRE.
– And your longings are so spiritual and high you
Know that nothing in this world can satisfy you.

TARTUFFE.
On the contrary, the quest for godliness

Shouldnae mak' us love the world the less.
It's His Creation cherms oor senses, which is only right
Because God made the world for oor delight.
The pleasure o' the sicht, say, o' some wummin who is
                                                    Really Nice
Is the nearest glimpse us pair, vile men get o' paradise
So, perfect creature, when you ken you are adored
Ken tae that in adorin' you I praise the Lord.
Aye, ma hert's transported, I am dazzled by your beauty!
Noo, at furst Ah hud tae ask masel, as wis ma duty,
Wis ah quite, quite shair this wee saicret tenderness
Wisnae mibbe yin o'Auld Nick's ploys, to land me in a mess?
Aye, Ah wiz feart you bein' sae . . . Nice Tae Lukk Ett
Wiz as a mote in ma e'e and Ah'd better pluck it
Oot, in case it staun atween me an' Salvation
As ony kinna stumblin' block. – Better, faur better than
                                                    Damnation
Wad be Ah'd flee fae you, ma yin Temptation.
Ah took it tae the Lord. He didny will sic deprivation.
He kennt Ah'd wrastled an' Ah'd wrastled wi ma passion,
Hoo Ah'd been up a' nicht on ma knees, fair lashin'
Masel' wi guilt, an' a' fur whit?
It could be reconcilt wi' discretion, Ah could gie wey tae it!
Ah ken, Ah ken, Ah've goat an awfy nerve –
Backward at comin' furrit as Ah am, Ah dinnae deserve
Ye'd show a hert o' flesh and bluid to me.
– Except you are kind – and God's aye guid to me!
Madam, Ah'm in your hauns, I'm tormentit!
Mak' me blissfu', peacefu' an' contentit!
Ah offer you this beatin' hert, so please yirsel'
Mak' me the happiest man on earth or dash ma hopes to Hell.

ELMIRE.

You are most . . . gall*ant*, but this declaration
Causes me great surprise, if not consternation –
You should have been a mite more guarded, sir, and thought
About the implications of such a plot.
You! Piety is your middle name!

TARTUFFE.

Oh aye, Ah'm mibbe holy, but Ah'm human a' the same.

It's you! Yir . . . celestial cherms are sae owerwhelmin'ly
tremendous

The hert kens nae reason, an' surrenders.
Noo, if such language micht sound strange Ah'll
Be the first tae admit it: Ah'm nae angel,
An' afore ye blame me, ye micht just as well
Blame yir ain enticin' weys, ya lovely Jezebel,
Yir comehither lukks, yir kennin' glances an' yir smiles.
Och, normally Ah'm proof against sicc female wiles.
F'r instance tak' the likes o' yir stepdaughter!

He shakes his head and MARIANNE *peeks out mad,
listening.*

Ah could pass lang 'oors alane wi her an' nae thought a
Ever even thinkin' o' her as a wummin!
Pair Wee Marianne! Nothin' worth bummin'
Aboot in the looks depertment as faur as Ah cin see!
An' yit she fairly loves hersel', it's 'Lukk ett me,
Ah'm jist gorgeous, Ah'm Ah no' the Bees' Knees?'
Fact is, some men urrny hard tae please.
Ony wee straight-up-and-doon skelf in a skirt's
Enough fur them – if she giggles an' flirts
An' wiggles an' flatters an' bats her een
An' greases up her lips wi' vaseline.
Skinnymalinky so-ca'd flappers canny haud a caunle
Tae a real wummin lik' you, yir too hoat tae haunle
– Ma angel, ma ice-maiden, ma fountain o' virtue!
Tak' peety on me an' ye cin bet yir shirt you
An' yir precious reputation will be safe wi' me.
A' they fly-boys an' gigolos, yi cin guarrantee
They'll boast an' brag aboot yi, they'll kiss an' tell
Wi' who, an' hoo minny times, an' hoo well!
Here's ma warnin' – an' it canny be too strongly worded –
What they kid-oan they worship, they mak' sordid.
But People Like Us, we're mair discreet
We're gey carefu' to guerd oor sweet
Ladies sweet nothin's, an' their sweet sumthin's tae –
– Well, oor *Ain* Good Names are, needless to say,
Things we must, at a' cost, tak' guid care y!
So, kiss me in confidence, dinny be wary!

An' Ah promise tae you, a' ma life lang, ma dear,
Love withoot Scandal, joy without Fear.

ELMIRE.

I hear what you're saying, but if I took the notion
To acquaint my husband with your . . . declared devotion
Wouldn't he feel betrayed by the man who so rewards him
For all the generous friendship he's shown towards him?

TARTUFFE.

Naw, naw, ye're faur too nice, you winnae!
Ah ken you ken yirsel' the flesh is weak, noo dinnae – !
Funn yirsel' a mirror, lukk lang an' deep in
An' mind that a man is jist a man – unless he's blin'.

ELMIRE.

Others might look at this differently . . .
But, on reflection, mibbe I'll go gently –
Not clype to my husband, let's say Ah'll
Keep mum about your proposition and betrayal
If – and only if – you do all you can
To hasten the wedding of Valère and Marianne
And openly denounce the power which would entrust
You with what belongs to someone else. It's unjust!
And . . .

Scene Four

MARIANNE *behind them is signalling delight at* ELMIRE*'s
wiles. As* VALÈRE *the foolhardy leaps out she ducks back out
of sight.*

VALÈRE.

I think it's time we spilt the beans!
I'm stuck here listening all the time this scene's
Unfolding and at first I can't believe my ears!
And then the penny drops. It clicks. Now here's
Our opportunity! Tartuffe's comeuppance!
He gave us it on a plate, I don't give tuppence

– Now he's blotted his copybook on every page –
For his chances of avoiding Orgon's rage.

ELMIRE.

No Valère. It is enough he mends his ways so
He deserves forgiveness by doing my say-so,
Remember? Propositions! A woman of the world'll just
          ignore them
And keep from her husband what'll only bore him.

MARIANNE *jumps out of hiding place.*

MARIANNE.

Valère's right!

ELMIRE (aside).

   Oh no!

VALÈRE.

     I'm sure you have your reasons
But now he's shown his colours, well the season's
Ripe for showing him his sun is set. It
Is all up, the party's over, sonny, don't forget it!
The cat's out of the bag, the truth's out of the closet
We'll open Orgon's eyes, Bob's your uncle, easy does it!
Don't beg or plead, Tartuffe, there is no use,
You've burnt your boats and cooked your goose.
Fate's dealt me a trump card. Oh ya beauty!
And I'll damn well play it. It is my duty.

ELMIRE.

Valère . . .

MARIANNE.

   Valère's right!

ELMIRE.

    Marianne . . .

VALÈRE.

      I must
Inform Orgon Tartuffe's betrayed his trust.

Scene Five

Enter ORGON.

MARIANNE.
Here's daddy now!

VALÈRE.
C'mere, sir, till we tell you
Something very rich! You should know how well you
Are paid back for your generosity.
Your kindness to certain strangers has earned a fine
reciprocity!
He reveals a zeal that's real, Tartuffe!
He wanted to betray you and I've got proof.
The worst bad black villain ever born's Tartuffe.
He would have had you wearing horns, Tartuffe
Would! I sat in that cupboard and I overheard
Him declare a filthy guilty passion to Elmire, every word!
Your easy-going wife would keep it secret. she doesn't want
To upset *you*, and she's so . . . tolerant.
But – the cheek of him! – I can't go along
With just-ignore-it! To shut up'd be wrong.

MARIANNE.
Valère's right!

ELMIRE.
The way I see it, the big mistake's
To worry one's old man with every passing pass that
someone makes.
I know I'm faithful, so why go in for sessions
Of No Kiss, But Still Tell All True Confessions?

Turning to MARIANNE.

You and your big mouth, miss, we'd have avoided this to-do
If I had more influence over you!

ORGON.
Whit? In the name o' God can this be possible?

TARTUFFE

> Yes, brither, it is – is this no terrible?
> Of a' sinners Ah am maist mizzrable.
> Ah cairry a ton weight o' stinkin' guilt that's truly horrible.
> Ah'm wicked, proud and fu' o' iniquitousness.
> Ah'm corrupted, Ah'm polluted, ma hale life is a mess.
> Thank you heaven! Ah see ye mean tae mortify me
> An' fur ma ain guid show me whit's fur me'll no go by me.
> Ah tell you, whether crime or error or jist faux-pas
> Ah'm guilty. Mea absolutely culpa.
> So tak' up erms, Orgon, an drive me fae yir door as
> Despised as rejectit as Nebbuchadnezzar on a' fours.
> Ah'm totally ashamed. Eftir a' you did for me
> Nae punishment's enough, hanging's too guid for me.

ORGON (TO VALERE.

> See! Ya snake-in-the gerss ye! Ye dampt *disease!*
> Hoo daur ye try an' blacken Him wi' yir damnable lees?

TARTUFFE.

> Orgon, Orgon, ye should listen to the boay!
> No' a bit o' malice in him, Ah'm shair he'd no enjoy
> Pittin' ye right aboot ma wrang-daein'.
> Dinny believe in me, d'ye ken whit yir sayin'?
> Don't jist trust ma fine exterior, Ah'd be a hypocrite
> If Ah kidded-oan ah wis perfect an' didny admit
> Ah'm capable o' vile treachery – which, God willin',
> Ah'll no' get away wi'. Unmask me as a villain.
> Fur Ah'm nothin' mair nor less, whitever folk think.
> The truth o' the maitter is : Ah stink.

TARTUFFE *sinks to his knees.*

ORGON.

> That's too much brither! (*To* VALÈRE.) Ya . . . Ya . . . take
> > back thae lies!

VALÈRE.

> It's that easy to pull the wool down over your eyes?

ORGON.

> Shut it ya – Och, brither, up ye get!
> Ya – och, see you, ya –

VALÈRE.

It's absurd! I've got proof, don't forget.

ORGON.

Wan mair word fae you an' Ah'll brekk yir boady!

TARTUFFE.

Dinnae, brither, dinnae, ah'll tak' the hale load y
Righteous anger on ma wicked shooders, d'ye no' see
Ah couldny staun tae see him suffer ower me?

ORGON.

Oh! ya –

TARTUFFE.

Forgi'e him, forgi'e him! If Ah've tae grovel in a midden
And beg on ma hauns and knees till –

ORGON.

Are you kiddin'?

Ya tyke, ye! See hoo guid he is!

VALÈRE.

Then you – ?

ORGON.

Don't dare abuse him!

Easy seein' yir motives, Ah ken how ye accuse him!
Yiz hate him! Ye dae, the hale dampt loat –
Wife, dochter, servants in wan big ploat
Tae discredit this . . . Saint here an' drive him away.
Ah'll keep him at my richt haun whitever yiz say.
Ah'll pit furrit the date, gi'e him ma dochter's haun'
Ah'm all for Tartuffe, an' Ah'll mak' yiz unnerstaun –

VALÈRE.

You'd force him on her, you're that twisted and bitter?

ORGON.

Aye, ya bliddy rascal, afore she kens whit's hit her
She'll be Mrs Tartuffe. This vera nicht.
That'll soart the loat o' yiz oot, a' richt!
Ah'll show yiz all Ah'm still the boss.
Doon oan yir knees you – Ah'll no argue the toss –

Dae it! Tak' it a' back, on yir bended knees,
And beg him to forgive you please.

VALÈRE.

Him? Who except for swindling's never done a thing for
you –

ORGON.

A stick! Gie's a stick, by God Ah'll swing for you!
Get oot o' here, an' never have the neck tae show yir face.

VALÈRE.

Awright, Ah'll go, but listen –

ORGON.

Get oot o' ma place!
Get oot all o' yiz, the quicker Ah see the back o' yiz
The better! Ah'll be revenged on the pack o' yiz!

ORGON *begins to swipe and swat everyone away except*
TARTUFFE, *who with one eye on this and a triumphant*
smirk he can't totally suppress sinks to his knees and begins
babbling more Lamentations.

TARTUFFE. *'They ravished the women in Zion and the maids*
in the cities of Judah! The elders have ceased from the gate
the young men from their music. Servants have ruled over
us and we have none that deliver us out of their hand.' '

Scene Seven

They are alone in quiet at last.

ORGON.

Tae insult yir Holy Name, ah'm black affronted!

TARTUFFE.

Heaven forgive them, the last thing Ah've wanted
Is tae be the inadvertant cause o' a' this fuss.
They wey they try an' blacken me, an' come atween us . . .

ORGON.

Dinnae!

TARTUFFE.

    The vera thocht o' sicc ungratefu'ness!
 . . . Tae come face to face lik' that wi' Man's Vile Black

               hatefu'ness

The horror! It's sic torture tae me
Ma hert's ower fu' tae talk, Ah'll dee!

ORGON *runs to the door and shouts after* VALÈRE.

ORGON.

Ya villain! (Tae think Ah let him go as well!)
Come back here till ah send ye tae hell!
Pey nae attention tae him, brither, dinnae fash yirsel –

TARTUFFE.

Naw, Ah've ootsteyed ma welcome, Ah cin tell.
Ah've caused a lot o' bother, and sich rows –
By faur the best thing fur it is Ah leave this house.

ORGON.

Whit? you're kiddin on –

TARTUFFE.

    They hate me!
They try 'n' arouse yir suspicions jist to bait me.

ORGON.

Them an' their rubbish, Ah cin dae withoot it!

TARTUFFE.

They'll persist wi' it, but, nae doot aboot it.
An' eftir the umpteenth time they've said it
Ah think ye'll begin tae gie their slanders credit.

ORGON.

Naw, brither. naw.

TARTUFFE.

    Aye brither, aye!
It's the wife that weers the breeks in here, that's why.

ORGON.

Nut at a'!

TARTUFFE.

>Let me leave here on the double,
Sharpish – afore they cause me further trouble.

ORGON.

>By God ye'll stey, Ah couldny five wi' sic a loss –

TARTUFFE.

>Och well ah suppose Ah'll huv tae bear ma cross
Hooever

ORGON.

>Eh?

TARTUFFE.

>A'richt, so be it!
But we'll huv tae soart things out . . . The way
Ah see it. . .Ah'll stey but Ah can only stey oan wan condtion.
We've tae no jist *be* but be-seen-to-be above suspicion.
So, tae stap, the waggin' tongues, upon ma life,
There's some'dy Ah'll shun lik' the plague – your wife.

ORGON.

>Naw ye willny, jist t'annoy them, jist fur spite
Ye'll see her morning noon an' night.
But that's no a'. Ah'll chinge ma will –
Soart ma cheeky bitch o' a daughter, if she's still
Under the illusion that she cin defy me,
Well, Ah've the whip haun', she'll be taught a lesson by me.
Ah'll mak' you ma yin an' only heir
So she'll mairry you or starve. An' furthermair
Why wait till Ah'm deid? Whit mair dae Ah want
Ah'll make everythin' ower tae you the now, by deed o'
>>covenant!
What di' you think o' that, eh, then?

TARTUFFE.

>Even so, Lord, Thy will be done, then . . . Amen.

ORGON.

>Pair sowell! Well, let's pit oor signatures on the page . . .
They'll be seeck! They'll be green! They'll burst wi' rage!

Music of a fanfare nature and jubiliant ORGON *insists on* TARTUFFE *signing, then exchanging papers and shaking hands. Of course* ORGON *loses his fountain pen to the villain as well, as off goes the poor dupe looking quite delighted with himself.* TARTUFFE *is too, now we have him alone and he can indulge it. He looks round, monarch of all he surveys, slides his hands over velvet upholstery, gloating, and sits down drumming his heels in delight and laughing like a maniac as the curtain falls.*

End of Act Three.

Interval.

ACT FOUR

Scene One

Enter CLÉANTE *to find* TARTUFFE *quiet, where we left him.*

CLÉANTE.

    Ah, very timely! Mr Tartuffe, upon my life
    Everybody's talking – the world and his wife
    Is quite scandalised by this – I hope it's untrue? –
    Otherwise it reflects most unfavourably on you.
    Maybe Valère's a hothead – perhaps mistaken, granted!
    – Certainly he was overquick accusing you in a way that
                            no one wanted
    But surely to goodness the Christian thing
    Is to pardon what seems beyond pardonning?
    Because of a wee falling-out he's banished, is it fair?
    The boy who was the future-son-in-law, the heir –
    Until Orgon capriciously went back on his word.
    People are, I repeat, outraged by it – it'd be absurd
    If it weren't so patently and painfully unjust.
    Here's my advice, sir, and you'll take it I trust?
    You're in a position to pour oil on troubled water
    Make it all hunky-dory again between father and daughter.
    A propos Valère . . . ask God to cleanse you of your
                        – understandable resentment
    And let the young ones get on with it in peace and
                              contentment.

TARTUFFE.

    Now it's ower and done wi' as faur as Ah'm concerned.
    I bear him nae grudge, Ah'm shair he's learned
    Repentance, is sorry, could bite his tongue et cetera.
    I forgive him, no bother – but Heaven kens it's better Ah
    Dinnae be seen tae have ony truck
    Wi' the young filla – you're richt – there's muck

In a' their minds an' rumours on their lips
An' their beady een are peeled for ither folk's slips
Or stumbles, backsliding's aff the straight and narra.
Turn the ither cheek? Ah'd be gled tae, but as far a
-S the warld's concerned it'd be as guid as pleading guilty.

                                                            How?

They'd reason it lik' this: Ah wis only actin' pally now
Because Ah wis feart o'ma just Accuser – that's how they'd
                                                    describe him
An' Ah wis only sufferin' him tae silence and bribe him.

CLÉANTE.

Mr. Tartuffe, that's a very colourful excuse.
A mite far-fetched this sophistry, now what's the use
Of taking on your feeble shoulders Heaven's interests.
Let Heaven punish who It likes, doesn't Heaven know best?
Vengeance is Mine Said the Lord – so let's leave him to it.
Remember, should He choose to forgive, then it's the right
                                                    thing to do it.
What should we care for the opinion of some mythical
                                                        'them'?
If 'they're' so petty-minded as condemn
A good deed, so twisted as misconstrue our motives
Then let 'us' obey Heaven, and if Heaven forgives –

TARTUFFE.

Ah tellt you I forgave him and I – don't you understand?
                                                        meant
Jist that. As is the Good Lord's Commandment,
Though Valère reviled and slandered me I forgive the blether.
But heaven kens it isny written we should live the-gether!

CLÉANTE.

And is it written sir, that on Orgon's whim
Valère be dispossessed and you should usurp him?
Taking his bride, her inheritance and his good name?
Accepting property to which you have no just claim?

TARTUFFE.

Ah jist maun trust that those who ken me best
Ken better than Ah'd act oot o' self interest.
A' the glisterin' riches in the warld mean nut a thing tae me.

Ah'm the last wan tae get dazzled by their glamourie
An' if, against ma inclinations, ah force masel
Tae tak this faither's insistit-oan gifts it's jist as well
Seein' as, otherwise, Ah'm very much feart it's bound to fa'
Inty wicked hauns that willny yase it well at a'!
But I, lik' the guid and faithfu' servant wi his talent, I will
                                                    yase it, if Ah can,
For the Glory o' God, the well-bein' o' ma fellow man.

CLÉANTE.
Better he misuse it and be answerable to God
Than you be – in error – suspected of fraud,
Sir!

TARTUFFE.
Would you look at the time, it's half past three!
A certain religious duty up the stairs, you'll have to be
                                                    excusing me –

Exits quickly.

CLÉANTE.
Em . . . !

Scene Two

Enter ELMIRE *and* DORINE *with weeping* MARIANNE.

DORINE.
                Help us sir, for pity's sake!
Lukk at the state she's in, we huv tae make –
Either by trickin' him or teachin' him sense
Her faither gie this up! Jine us in defence
O' fair play an' true love against this mess
O' maister's. Sich unhappiness.

Scene Three

Enter ORGON.

ORGON.
  Och! A' here thegither? That's sweet.

  To MARIANNE.

  Somethin' in these papers, hen, that's right up your street.

MARIANNE.
  Father, in the name of anythin' that's sacred to your heart,
                                            or moves you,
  For the sake of Heaven, and your own daughter who
                                            loves you,
  I beg you, daddy, please, please, you gave me life.
  Don't render it a misery to me by making me the wife
  Of a man who to even think of makes my flesh to crawl.
  Must I give up my last sweet hope for once and all?

  ORGON *is moved. Aside, to himself.*

ORGON.
  Be firm! Ever since she wis a toddler she could wrap ye
                                            roon her pinkie!

MARIANNE.
  I'm not put-out *you* love him, I think he
  Must deserve it, if you think so, fine.
  Give him all your money and add what's mine,
  It doesn't matter to me, I present
  My last trinket, take it, give it with my consent
  From the bottom of my heart. And God he
  Knows that all I ask's you don't give away my body.
  And if I can't marry that one person I love so much
  Then let me die a maiden, untouched . . .

  *She has bowed her head during this last speech so she
  doesn't see that* ORGON *is reaching out about to give way
  to her, softened utterly.*

MARIANNE.

> Let me turn Catholic! In God's honour, He
> Bids me live my days out in a nunnery.

ORGON.

> Turn whit! Ah think you must be makin' fun o'me!
> Ya *get* ye! Ye'll get ye to no nunnery!
> Did yir Daddy hear ye say a Catholic Convent? Hih? Nae
>   wunner he
> Is *forced* tae huv tae run yir life fur ye.
> Get oan yir feet! Ah don't know whit tae say!
> Maks 'yir flesh creep' diz he? Oh aye!
> There's ower much concentration on 'the flesh' that's why.
> That's an end tae it! Forget the flesh's vile gratification,
> Mortify yirsel, mairry him an' avoid damnation.

DORINE.

> But whit –

ORGON.

>   You haid yir tongue! God's truth!
> Ah'll . . . Ah'll . . . Jist shut yir mooth.

CLÉANTE.

> For what it's worth, can I just put in a word –

ORGON.

> Ha-ha! Your advice, brither, is the best Ah've heard
> Ah mean it! Honestly Ah'm grateful for it –
> Forgive me though if this once Ah ignore it!

ELMIRE.

> Enough! I just don't know what to say
> Except your wilful blindness takes my breath away.
> You must be literally bewitched, quite honestly,
> To deny the truth of what occurred today.

ORGON.

> Ah! Well, Ah'm faur fae blin', unfortunately fur you!
> Valère 's a nice lukkin' young fella, eh? – sich as you're
>   partial to?
> Favouratism mak's ye that bit lenient, ye didny want tae
>   contradict him

When he tried to play his durty trick wi' Tartuffe for a victim.
– But of coorse ma lovely wife would have been *faur* mair
upset
If a man had *really* made advances tae ma innocent wee pet.

ELMIRE.

You wanted me to prudishly pretend to be offended!
I simply laughed it off. My honour's easily defended
Because I'm quite secure in it, my dear.
Some of these spitfires and hysterics doth protest too much,
I fear.

I find a civilised and cool-but-firm rebuff
Deters unwanted attentions effectively enough.

ORGON.

Nevertheless there's naebody gonny tak' a len o' me!

ELMIRE.

Hell's teeth! Alright, we'll make you see.

ORGON.

See?

ELMIRE.

Uh-huh, see.

ORGON.

Well, Ah'd be seein' things.

ELMIRE.

Righto!

Suppose I said I'd prove that it was so?

ORGON.

Ah'd say that was a loady –

ELMIRE.

What a man! Enough!
Before your very eyes I'll make him do his stuff.
Get him to come here!

DORINE.

He isny daft, he
Likely willny let you catch him, he's too crafty –

ELMIRE.

> Hurt someone where he loves, that's how to really cause
> > confusion!
> Self-love leads easily to self delusion.
> So send him down and leave us for a bit –

Shoos out CLÉANTE, MARIANNE *and* DORINE.

Scene Four

ELMIRE.

> Quick! Pull over that table and get under it.

ORGON.

> How?

ELMIRE.

> God help me, so that you can hide.

ORGON.

> Why in below here?

ELMIRE.

> > . . . If ever a woman had her patience solely tried
> Never mind! A foolproof scheme and you shall be its judge.
> Under this table. Keep quiet. Don't budge.

ORGON.

> Ah look as if Ah'm that daft! O.K . . . Under there . . .

He goes.

ELMIRE.

> Sweetheart, you'll see me acting sort of strangely I declare
> I'm going to do a thing I've never done before in all my life!
> Now don't let it shock you, dear, to see a new side of your
> > wife.
> Remember 'ends and means'. . . and so on . . . and since you
> Refuse to take me at my word I must convince you –
> So don't cast it up after! You mustn't disparage

ELMIRE.

    My motives, dearest, if I sort of encourage –
    By buttering him up – you'll see me flirt somewhat and
                                        flatter . . .

    Oh a dirty trick perhaps, but, no matter
    It was *he* proposed outrageous things to *me!*
    So I'll encourage full expression of his lust and vanity.
    Now it's up to you to call a halt – you'd be more than an
                                    accessory
    If you let this odious charade last one minute longer than is
                                    necessary

    Husht!

Scene Five

Enter TARTUFFE.

TARTUFFE.

       They tell me that you wish to speak with me?

ELMIRE.

    I do, I do indeed, in secrecy . . .
    Shut the door. That cupboard! We don't want noseyparkers
                                     check!

    No repetitions of that last fiasco, we got a right rid neck!
    Valère and Marianne landed us right in it, I was worried
                                     for you!

    I tried to shut him up, I didn't know what to do . . .
    I was that vexed at them . . . *confused*, that was why it
    Never even occurred to me to deny it!
    But all's well that ends well, better by far
    My husband himself dismissed it and here we are!
    Alone. With his blessing. Trusted. I'm hoping
    (I blush) we can hide our love affair out in the open?

TARTUFFE.

    Our love a – whit? Madam, this efternoon
    Ye hud me dancin' tae a different tune.

ELMIRE.

>Dear Tartuffe, you don't know women, you're so innocent!
>A refusal like that! You surely never thought I meant
>It? We women struggle so with modesty when we transgress
>But you know that we say 'no' when we mean 'yes'!
>I spoke a dutiful refusal, as I know you realise,
>With a butter-wouldn't-melt mouth, but come-to-bed eyes.
>– I ask you: would I have tried to shush Valère?
>Would I have listened to you so long? And what do you infer
>From the fact I tried to force you to renounce the marriage
>But that I basically wanted to encourage
>You to keep your love intact, and all-for-me,
>Because I was literally green with jealously?

TARTUFFE.

>It's the sweetest thing on earth – thanks be tae heaven above
>– Tae hear honey love-words fae someb'dy that ye love.
>Ah never tasted sicc a precious thing afore –
>Ma yin thocht is tae mak' happy the wummin Ah adore.
>But – haud oan ma foolish hert! – I hae a lingerin' suspicion
>– Noo I micht be wrang, but pit yersel in ma position –
>Whit if Ah break aff the weddin' because Ah believe
>That you want ma love, then yi laugh up yir sleeve
>An' it turns oot it wiz jist a ploy?
>Ah can't 'just trust' in tender words till Ah enjoy
>Warm livin' breathin' tenderness atween us baith.
>Kiss me! Quickly! In token of good faith.

ELMIRE *coughs a warning at hidden* ORGON.

ELMIRE.

>Whit! I emm don't think we need move so fast –
>Too soon spent kisses never last!
>I promise all the happiness of which you dream's
>Around the corner, if you don't push it to extremes . . .

TARTUFFE.

>It's kennin' ma ain worthlessness mak's me doot
>That you could ever love me, so withoot
>You prove yir love in no uncertain fashion
>Ah canny go a' the wey wi yir words o' passion.

ELMIRE.

Goodness! I love you so it gives me palpitations.
My heart is pounding with agitation
Of seeing that my churning feelings don't burst their dam!
You mustn't take advantage, see how weak I am . . .
A mere woman led astray by the man on whom she depended!
It'd be quite wrong, heaven would be offended.

TARTUFFE.

Leave it tae me tae square it wi Heaven.

ELMIRE.

It'd be a mortal sin, we'd never be forgiven –

TARTUFFE.

Heaven forbids certain things, oh aye, bit we'd better
Mind we're enjoined tae follow the spirit o' the law and no
the letter
Under certain circumstances these . . . gratifications that
I mention
Micht be richt – accordin' tae Purity o' Intention.
And by God Ah'm gonny pure – !! . . . Ma *intention*s are pure
So on ma heid be it, ye cin rest secure –
My that's an awfy cough!

ELMIRE.

Yes! It's ticklish!

TARTUFFE.

You want a wee boiling tae sook, or a bit o' lickerish?

ELMIRE.

It's tiresome right enough, Ah canny seem to shift it.
My chest's that congested! Take mair than liquorice to lift it!

She pats at her cleaveage for TARTUFFE*'s benefit, coughs
for her husband's.*

TARTUFFE.

Quite a chest right enough . . .

ELMIRE.

Och! It's got me demented!

TARTUFFE.

Oh Ah know whit ye mean. Hmm. Well, Ah hope Ah've

prevented

You from being a victim of a silly scruple,
Let me lead ye, be ma mistress, be ma pupil,
Let me show ye it's the world and its durty mind
Disapproves o' love! God isny so unkind!

ELMIRE *has a fit of coughing.*

ELMIRE.

Well it seems I must give in –
Lie with you in secrecy, and in sin.
What my old man doesn't *see* , whether it's wrong or right's
Certainly not going to cause him any sleepless nights.
Since certain people don't believe in idle words, Mr Tartuffe
It seems a bit of action'll show you proof,

Yelling.

Like they say, on your head be it.

Lies back on the table.

TARTUFFE (*undoing trousers and rolling up her skirt*).
At last! Noo let's get on wi' it!
Noo Ah take it on masel, as you'll soon see –

ELMIRE *pushes him off.*

ELMIRE.

Is ma husband in the passage? Check and see!

TARTUFFE.

Is he in the whit? Never heed yir man,
We'll pull a fast one on him if anybody can!
An richt afore his nose. Clues! They're just ignored!
He's satisfied our only intercourse is . . . quite above board.

TARTUFFE *bangs out last on the table.*

ELMIRE.

Nevertheless I'm just not too sure where he is exactly.
Check it out for me. . and mibbe that'll relax me . . .

TARTUFFE *complies with a roar of frustration.*

Scene Six

ORGON *comes out from under the board.*

ORGON.
Ah'm – Ah jist canny – who'd've guessed he'd . . .
Whit an abominable man, Ah'm flabbergasted!

ELMIRE.
Out so soon? Get back! To avoid any confusion
We'll go all the way to its logical conclusion.

ORGON.
Ah'll see him in Hell! Ma wife! Oh no.

ELMIRE.
Now it isn't necessarily so!
Misjudging people can be very nasty
And the last thing you ought to be is overhasty.

Scene Seven

She's pushed ORGON *to the floor,* TARTUFFE *doesn't see
him, pushes* ELMIRE *back, drops his trousers.*

TARTUFFE.
Ssh! . . . There's neither hide nor hair . . . On top o' me!

ORGON *leaps out.*

ORGON.
My wife! My God! It's daylight robbery . . .
You'd marry ma dochter and . . . and . . . My wife!
Ah've aye had ma suspicions but . . . but never in ma life
Have Ah seen sich . . . sich . . . Oh, Treacherous Stuff,
Sir! You've broke ma hert, Ah've seen enough . . .

ELMIRE.
  I didn't want to, it was a . . . bit
  Below the belt but then you asked for it!

TARTUFFE.
  Whit? D'y' really think . . .

ORGON.
                              Ya bliddy louse!
  Nut wan word. Get out ma house.

ELMIRE.
  Ye talk as ye were the maister! Get oot o'whit?
  Whose hoose? It's *ma* hoose, Ah'll mind ye o' it.
  – By Christ ye've gone too far.
  Ma 'oor is come. My power. Ma risin' star
  Is in the Heavens. Ah'll punish ye!
  O they shall eat bitter gall who tried to banish me!

He exits.

Scene Eight

ELMIRE *manages to get out a forced snigger.*

ELMIRE.
  'They shall eat bitter gall!' The cheek of it!

ORGON.
  Shut yir stupit face, it's nuthin tae laugh ett!

ELMIRE.
  Why?

ORGON.
           I see my fault. I've ruined us all.
  The deed of covenant . . . My house shall fall.

ELMIRE.
  The deed of what?

ORGON.

                  It's done. Consumatum est.
Whit am Ah sayin'? A wolf dressed
Up in sheep's claes. That villain's capers
Were jist tae deliberately dae me oot the Secret Papers!

Exit ORGON *in terrible state.*

ACT FIVE

Scene One

ELMIRE *stands sobbing, adjusting her disarrayed clothing, reliving the disgust of* TARTUFFE's *hands on her.*

ELMIRE.
> Dorine! Dorine! Oh why's there never anybody when I want
> Them? Help me . . . Oh God . . . Cléante!

CLÉANTE *enters leading a totally shattered* ORGON.

CLÉANTE.
> Now we have to think it out, it seems to me
> We better analyse alternatives, look at it logically.
> What steps? What losses? What possible gains –

ORGON.
> Above all it's the case, that briefcase contains
> Somethin' that could mean the end.
> Argas brought me certain papers. Argas, my friend,
> The one who was betrayed. Before he fled
> He asked me would Ah guard them or his head
> Would roll. He trusted me you understand.

CLÉANTE.
> Why then did you entrust this to another hand?

ORGON.
> Ah meant it for the best. It was from a sense
> Of mibbe no bein' worthy o' this trust Ah went, in confidence,
> An' tellt the hale tale tae that bliddy rascal.
> His argument wiz this: 'This task'll
> Be much better done gin ye gie the boax to me, Tartuffe.
> Then ye cin at yince be shair it's safe ablow yir roof
> An' at the same time – should snoopers come – deny
> Ye huv it in yir possession, with not wan word o' a lie.

CLÉANTE.

It looks like you are in it up to here.
This misplaced trust, this deed of gift are both, I fear,
Things you may live long to regret . . .
Still, he's got you by the short-and-curlies don't forget!
So the worst thing we can do is irritate him –
I wish there was some mollifying subterfuge that might
placate him . . .

ORGON.

May God damn an' blast an' pit a pox on pious folk.
Ah loathe an' detest them they gie me the boke.
Ah'll 'In-the-name-o'-the-faither-son-an'-Holy-Ghost' them!
Ah'll hunt them tae Hell, Ah'll roast them!

CLÉANTE.

Orgon, Orgon, is yon no just like you?
Nae moderation in ye, man, you overdo
It all and lose the rag, you make
Yourself ridiculous! You see your big mistake,
You – and you're not the first one – got took in by a fake.
But all pious people aren't imposters for goodness sake!
Oh the con-man may have a silver tongue, but nevertheless
Our better judgement should be a litmus test for phoniness
And if in doubt we ought to hedge our bets
And steer a somewhat middle-course that lets
Time teach us who we ought to trust.
But still I think we ought to err, if err we must,
As you have erred – by being vulernable and risking
Loving your fellow man in a way that's only Christian.

[*Molière Scene Two cut.*]

Scene Three

Enter PERNELLE, MARIANNE, ELMIRE *and* DORINE.

ORGON.

Oh naw! Here's ma mither, oh dear oh dear!

PERNELLE.
   Whit's the maitter, whit's a' this Ah hear?

ORGON.
   Fine sichts Ah saw wi ma ain twa een
   That proved hoo weel peyed back Ah've been
   Fur a' ma guidness. Furst Ah took him in,
   Fed him, claithed him – if he'd been ma kin
   Ah couldny have done mair fur him.
   Ah gied him ma ain dochter sac weel did Ah care fur him.
   An' – oh the villainy! – Ah trust him wi' ma life
   An' the devil tries tae seduce ma wife.
   No content wi' this, he wants ma total ruination.
   Each weel-meant hansell, each gift, deed or donation
   Ah gied him oot the goodness o' ma hert
   He wants tae yase against me tae ootsmert
   An' swick me oot ma hale estate – you're
   Richt, Ah'm a fule tae masel', it is ma nature–
   He'll deprive me o' ma last crust o' breid an' butter
   An pit me whaur Ah picked him up, the gutter.

DORINE.
   The sowell.

PERNELLE.
                This Ah don't believe, Ah'll
   Never accept That Man could be sae evil.

ORGON.
   How?

PERNELLE.
          Guid Folk are ayeweys envied by the ither
   Soart, believe me.

ORGON.
                How d'ye mean, eh, Mither?

PERNELLE.
   Awfy strange shenanigans ablow this roof.
   Easy seein' that they a' hate Tartuffe.

ORGON.
   Ah'll 'shenanigans' him! Whit justification cin you offer –

PERNELLE.

Pure spite! An' aye the innocent must suffer.

The jealous may perish – lik'

Ah says when you were wee –

But The Auld Green Eyed Monster Will Never Ever Dee.

ORGON.

Whit huz that tae dae wi' it? Who's jealous?

PERNELLE.

The loat o' them. Made the hale thing up. Pure malice.

ORGON.

Ah seen it wi' ma ain twa een! God gi'e me strength . . .

PERNELLE.

Scandalmongerin' slanderers wid go tae ony length.

ORGON.

Huv yi loast yir senses a' thegither?

Ah seen him. Richt afore ma very eyes. D'ye hear me mither?

Ah saw it all. Whit cin Ah say? Must Ah shout

At the tap o'ma voice afore ye tak' in whit Ah'm talkin' about?

Ah saw him. Ah saw him wi' these twin undimmed orbèd

optics

I perceived the visual proof to satisfy a school of sceptics.

PERNELLE.

You shouldny judge by appearances you know!

Jist 'cos ye thocht ye saw somethin' disnae prove that it

wis so.

ORGON.

Gie me strength!

PERNELLE.

We're prone to suspicion, son – it's gey

Easy tae tak' somethin' the wrang wey!

ORGON.

Coorse, it wis jist his guid deed o' the day, and how,

Tae try 'n seduce Ma Wife –

PERNELLE.

Now, now!

Just cause afore ye accuse folk, or it isny fair!
Never open yir mooth in anger until ye urr quite shair.

ORGON.

Shair! Should Ah huv jis stood by while he dragged her
Doon tae his vile Level, upped her skirt and – shairly
Ye dinna think Ah'd accuse the man unfairly?

PERNELLE.

Ah jist cannot accept he is to blame
For whit you say! Pair man, it is a shame –

ORGON.

Enough! If you were not ma mither, Ah'd . . .
Ah'd . . . Ah'd Ah-don't-know-whit, you make me that mad!

DORINE.

It's jist your Just Desserts, it shouldny grieve you.
You wouldny believe us, so why should she believe you?

CLÉANTE.

We're wasting time on all this piffle! What your forgettin's
How daft it is to fight amongst ourselves while danger
threatens.

ELMIRE.

Danger! The man's a mere balloon! In short
Even he couldn't be that blatant, he'd be laughed out of court!

CLÉANTE.

I don't think we can afford to be confident in our position.
If he wants to get legal he's got plenty ammunition.
Many's the man with a case less cut-and-dried
Has bankrupted another with the law on his side.
We should've kept in his good books at all cost and not
Pushed him so far – with the cards that *he's* got!

ORGON.

That's true. Ah ken. But it wisnae a maitter
O being in control when Ah seen that traitor –

CLÉANTE.

I know, I know! I wonder is there any use
In negotiating, somehow, between you some sort of truce?

ELMIRE.

    I'd never have dangled myself like a carrot
    If I'd known exactly the stick *he* had to wield and how far it
    All might go, oh –

Knock knock knock pause knock knock knock at the door.

ORGON.

                 Whit next? Who the hell can that be?
    Awa' an tell them yir maister's in nae fit state tae talk
                              tae anyb'dy.

Scene Four

MR LOYAL *puts his foot in the door as* DORINE *opens it.*
Is heard off.

LOYAL.

    Mr Orgon? Live here, diz he?
    Can I have a word, please –

DORINE.

                    Maister's busy.

LOYAL (*entering*).

    I'd be the last person to intrude
    On a man in his ain hame. Yir maister should
    Be quite pleased tae hear whit Ah huv tae say.
    Nothin' he'll feel put-oot aboot, anyway . . .

DORINE.

    And yir name, sir?

LOYAL.

                On behalf of Mr. Tartuffe, I would
    Like a wee word wi' your good maister, f'r his own good.

DORINE.

    He's a man who seems to be wan o' nature's gentlemen
    Here fae Who-D'ye-Cry-Him-Again?
    – On business which he says'll please ye.

CLÉANTE.

Wonder what he wants? Best if he sees you

ORGON.

Mibbe he's here tae redd it up an' sort it
Hoo cin his favour best be courtit?

CLÉANTE.

Now no resentment, keep your hair on, and in his eyes
Such moderation might encourage him to compromise.

LOYAL.

Good day to you and yours, maister, your servant I'm sure.
Herm to those that'd herm ye, and may Heaven secure
Every blessin' on yir house and name and, don't forget,
We never died o' winter yet.

ORGON.

This filla couldnae be mair civil in his greetin'!
Mibbe eftur a' we can hae some kinna haulf wey meetin' . . .

LOYAL.

Ah meet ye at last, sir. There wis naebody Ah'd raither
Dae business wi than your auld dad. Aye! Ah kennt yir faither.

ORGON.

Ah thocht Ah kennt yir face but tae ma shame
Ah don't think ah cin place yir name . . . ?

LOYAL.

My name is Loyal – and don't get huffy sir
When Ah tell you Ah am, by profession, a Sherriff's Officer
Who has for forty years held this position, tae ma credit,
And is here today to serve you wi' a writ.

ORGON.

A whit?

LOYAL.

Noo, noo dinny get excited!
Dinnae loss the heid! That's no how wrongs git righted.
This is nothing but a mandate of citation
Ordering you leave your abode or habitation,
Aforesaid, without delay, with no right of appeal.

ORGON.

Leave ma hoose? Please God this isny real

LOYAL.

Noo, sir, yir hoose, grounds an' every stick o' furniture
                                        ablow this roof
As ye ken very well, belangs, nae question, tae Tartuffe.
Signed and sealed sir, in this document which Ah canny
                                        help admirin'
For its legal phrasin'. It's – in layman's terms – cast iron.

DORINE.

Pit a man oot his ain hoose? That's great, you're
Obviously Loyal by name, hih, an' Loyal by nature.

LOYAL.

Noo Ah dinny see why he tak's it personal an'lukks a'victim
An' longfaced aboot it! Because Ah'm here tae evict him
In as pleasant a manner as is, under difficult circumstances,
                                        possible.
Ah asked tae deliver this personally, because ah thocht
                                        it'd be terrible
If, no' bein' (as Ah like tae think o' masel') a freen' o'
                                        the fam'ly
The deliverin' officer micht *no'* go softly-softly an'
                                        approach it calmly . . .

ORGON.

There is nae saftenin' o' the cruelest blow.
Tae pit a man oot his ain hame!

LOYAL.

                            Ah'll gi'e ye time ye know.
Ah'll suspend proccedin's, under ma right o' discretion,
And wait till the morra afore Ah take possession.
Okey-dokey. Oh . . . Ah'll hiv tae come an' spend the night
Wi aboot ten o' ma men, ken . . . but they'll be polite!
Nane o' yir rough-stuff, ye'll no ken they're there.
Coorse, ye'll hae tae haun' ower the keys. Tae me. Bit
                                        Ah'll tak' care
There'll be nut a dicky-bird tae disturb yir last night's rest.
But the morn's mornin'. The flittin'. It'd be for the best

If ye'd a' a wee hand-bag packed wi some personal effects,
Items o' essential clothin', etcetra . . . Ah hope naebody

suspects

Tartuffe o' itemising every last crumb or lentil –
Help yirsel' oot the larder! An' tak the odd geegaw o'

sentimental

Value – jist check it oot wi me furst – we'll no be hard.
Ma men are a' big strong boays, they'll help ye cairry!

Well, a bodyguard

Joab lik' theirs means big broad shooders come in

convenient . . .

Now, as Ah'm shair ye appreciate, Ah've been very lenient
An' treated you, *Ah* feel, mair than fairly.
So Ah cin expect, in return, a bit o' co-operation, shairly?

ORGON.

Co-operwhit? Ah mibbe dinny hae a bean
Tae cry my ain, but Ah tell you Ah mean
Tae git revenge. Ah'd gie a'ma wealth-that-was
Tae brekk yir jaw and kick yir –

CLÉANTE.

Wheesht, you'll make things worse –

DORINE.

Because

Ah'm a wummin doesny mean ma fingers urny itchin' fur a

stick,

Or Ah dinny notice hoo yir erse is the right shape fur a kick!

LOYAL.

Because yir a wummin disny mean that yir above the law.
Git tae vote, eh? Well, ye git tae go tae jile an a'.

CLÉANTE.

Enough of all this! Stop it. Cease
Serve your damned paper sir, and leave us in peace.

LOYAL.

Cheerio. For the present. May God give you grace.

Exit LOYAL.

ORGON.

May he damn you and the man who sent you to this place.

Scene Five

ORGON.

Wis Ah right or wis Ah wrang, eh Mither?
This treachery must convince ye o' the ither,
An' shairly even you'll admit at last thit –

PERNELLE.

Ah've seen it a'. Ah'm flabbergastit.

DORINE.

I'm sure ye shouldny blame him, this is proof
O' hoo benevolent is Mister Tartuffe.
The sowell relieved you o' your money
Because you'd be better off if you hudna any

ORGON.

Haud yir tongue! If Ah've tellt yi wance, for pity's sake.

CLÉANTE.

Let us decide what course tae take . . .

ELMIRE.

As far as I can see the whole thing's preposterous!
Such blatant injustice can be no threat to us!
If he were successful it'd cause a public stink.
Or else the law's a far greater ass, even, than I think.

Scene Six

Enter VALÈRE.

VALÈRE.

This is very urgent, or, believe me, I'd not disturb you.
I've just heard something which will perturb you
I'm sure, as it did me. A certain friend of mine, in fact
Someone who knows you too, in defiance of the Official
Secrets Act

At great risk to himself, leaked certain information
On the strength of which a permanent vacation
Might seem more than desirable. Don't pack, just go.
Certain charges have been brought, you ought to know,
Against you specifically by that bloody imposition
And imposter who you loved. Murmurs of sedition
Were poured in the ears of certain high heid yins,
Papers produced belonging to a Known State Criminal
                                   whose allegiance
Is *not* to our democratic way of life, to say the least.
Tartuffe maintains you harboured this beast,
Helped him escape, concealed for him a certain object
– Namely that box of documents – as no loyal subject
Of Mr. Prince or our proud nation ever would.
I don't know the ins-and-outs but there's a warrant out, it
                                   could
Be that you're accused of a very serious crime indeed.
And, all the better to arrest you, Tartuffe's going to lead
The arresting officer here to execute his
Warrant and fulfil his duties.

CLÉANTE.

He's got all the ammunition he needs. That's how the
                                   impostor
Will strip you of everything and make himself master.

ORGON.

I tell you that man is a vile, vile creature . . .

VALÈRE.

By God you're right! Tartuffe, I hate your
Stinking guts, let me get one punch, I'll kill you –

MARIANNE.

Valère shut up and save my father, will you?

VALÈRE.

Yes. Quick. Delay is fatal, it's all arranged,
A car outside with its engine running, I've changed
As much currency as I could possibly muster.
They're hot on our heels but we'll be faster.
There's a time to fight, but now's a time to run.

We'll get you to some safe place-in-the-sun.
No arguments, father, I'm going too.
If it's to the ends of the earth, I'll see it through.

ORGON.

My boay, should Ah survive a' this Ah owe it
A' tae you. Ah'm sorry. Ah'm thankfu'– but Ah canny show it
In ony usefu'wey unless Heaven grant
Me someday the chance to gi'e you a' ye want.
Tak' guid care noo, all o' yiz –

CLÉANTE.

                              Quick, run
We'll see to everything that must be done.

Last Scene

TARTUFFE.

Tooch-tooch, Ah widnae get a jildy oan . . .
New ludging's ready for you and you alone . . .
You're for the jile, by order o' Mr. Prince hissel'.

ORGON.

This is the unkindest cut o' all.
Ya devil, the worst thing I could o' askit
Fur, this fairly tak's the biscuit.

TARTUFFE.

In the name o' Heaven, Ah jist let this vile attack
'N abuse roll aff, watter aff a duck's back.

CLÉANTE.

How moderate! I do admire such restraint.

VALÈRE.

He bandies Heaven's name aboot, but holy he aint!

TARTUFFE.

Neither Heaven nor me's bothered by yir dog's abuse.
Ah'm only keen tae serve my country and be o' use.

MARIANNE.

> 'Serve your country.' Tall order, but then
> Aren't you the best and noblest citizen!

TARTUFFE.

> Tall order nut-at-all! An honour, a glory, tae obey
> The authority an' power that sends me here the day.

ORGON.

> Ungratefu' tyke-ye, tae bite the haun that fed ye.
> D'ye mind the muck and stinkin' poverty fae which Ah led ye?

TARTUFFE.

> Mind it? Sir, ye were mair than generous.
> But affairs o' state are a loat bigger than us!
> An duty demands Ah sacrifice ma personal feelin's
> – Ah tell you, withoot a qualm, nae double dealin's,
> Ah'd name names. Ma Mither Hirsel', if Ah suspect it
> She was now or had ever been infectit
> Wi' the vile contagion o' insurrection –
> Well, ma duty would be tae refuse her protection.

ELMIRE.

> Hypocrite!

DORINE.

> An awfy tricky tongue on him! The felly
> Jist turns whit folk haud sacred inty his moral umb'relly

CLÉANTE.

> Fair enough! But is this zealous loyalty you talk about
> And are (excuse me) so cock-of-the-walk about –
> Is indeed this Pure and Perfect Thing
> Where did it hide itself as you were propositioning
> – To put it *very* mildly – this man's wife?
> I've never heard such fatuous hypocrisy in all my life.
> To denounce him somehow did not occur
> Until he caught you with her
> And, of course, was forced to send you away.
> Now he *had* given you all his property, but I don't say
> You should have let this seduce you from your duty.
> Yet why oh why – et tu Brute, isn't it a beauty?–
> Did your dexterous right hand take and take and take

>While the sinister other stabbed him in the back, and
>>no mistake!

TARTUFFE.
>Officer, this damnable racket is getting on ma nerves.
>We've a guilty man here, gie him whit he deserves.

OFFICER.
>You're absolutely right, Sir, the sooner we get on wi' it,
>The sooner we'll be ower and done wi' it.
>Mister Tartuffe: I arrest you in the name of the law.
>Your cell's a' swept oot an' ready for you an a' . . .

TARTUFFE.
>Who, me?

OFFICER.
>>Aye you.

TARTUFFE.
>>Why? Tae the jile . . . ?

OFFICER.
>I don't owe you any explanations, sir, but while
>I don't *need* to tell you nuthin', a' right, I will.
>Mr. Prince hates those who would do justice ill.
>Mr. Prince's most hated enemy is fraud.
>Mr. Prince's eyes, sir, like the Eyes of God,
>Can see inty the depths of the human heart.
>Mr. Prince is proof against the con-man's art.
>Not wan to fall for any cock and bull,
>Nor tae let nae silvertongued pattermerchant pull the wool.
>He's a reasonable man, and wan no' lightly swayed.
>His judgements are sound, and balanced, and weighed.
>Men o' worth bask in his everlasting favour,
>But forgive an act o' treachery? No sir, never!
>So: this man convince him? It couldny happen.
>– Be up a loat earlier, son, to catch him nappin'–
>Seen right through him from the start!
>Hoo black, and vile, and twisted, wis his heart.
>Wance alertit, Intelligence exposed him as a latterday
>Notorious known criminal who, under anither identity,
>Investigations revealed. was guilty of profanity,

Indency, gross moral turpitude and high treason.
Well Mr. Prince had a' ready been gonny punish him – if
                              fur nae ither reason
Than fur his disloyalty in tryin' tae dae you herm,
An' noo thae ither crimes, a list's long as yir erm!
So I'm here under strict instructions tae let the evil-doer
Go a'the wey wi'his villainy – sort o' a-jong provocatoo-er'
As the French cry it – and shair enough
Did he no condemn his-sel' oot o' his ain mooth? No hauf!
So: I'm ordert a' threat o' eviction be removed fae yir heads,
I've tae take this 'Deed o' Gift' rip it inty shreds.

He does so.

Just men who love the Government needny fear the Law.
Is a contract worth the paper that it's written oan? Nut at a'!
Thank God Good.Government's Sovereign Power can aye
                              arrange it
that if a law isny servin' justice, well . . . they can change it.
Therefore if Orgon was Too Good, and got gulled
By This Wan – the contract is annulled.
Mr. Prince is happy to pardon your . . . wee indiscretion
Wi' the boax of papers – if you've learned yir lesson!
Well, whit's a wee paccadillo compared to the loyalty
You showed him in former times, your defence of royalty
In the face of the forces of lawlessness?
The Monarchy's mibbe All Powerful, but nevertheless
Its memory for a Good Deed is much longer
Than it is for wee mistakes! The Good is stronger!

DORINE.
Good God Almighty!

PERNELLE.
                    We can breathe again

ELMIRE.
It's over . . .

MARIANNE.
                    Never thought I'd see the day when –

MARIANNE *and* VALÈRE *kiss.*

ORGON.

Ya vile an' Vicious traitor –

CLÉANTE.

>Don't descend to his level!

Let Heaven be the one to punish the devil.
Remorse will have to come from him and him alone
When he looks into his blackheart and sees his own
Vileness, owns up to it in genuine repentance.
Then our lenient Prince may modify his sentence.
Orgon, go to Mr. Prince and throw yourself at his feet,
Thank God and him it's clemency and not revenge that's

>sweet.

ORGON.

You are right, sir. As ye were a' alang.
Ah'll tell Mr. Prince an a' ma faimily: Ah wis wrang.
But, this duty done, there'll be happier still!
Valère and Marianne wad mairry? Well, they will!
And may they never forget the lesson Ah hae learnt the day.

DORINE.

We'll be happy ever eftir. And the band will play!

End.

Glossary

Note: My *Tartuffe* was set in the early 1920s (one production did very successfully place it as late as 1953) among a small-town bourgeoisie. Therefore this play is vigorously and unashamedly in the kind of Scots that might well need a glossary for the non-Scots reader – who would have no difficulty whatsoever if watching a live production. *Miseryguts*, being set in the here and now – and among posh folk in the capital too – still has plenty of Scots, often ironically used by the speakers, among its clichés, buzzwords, Americanisms and casual profanity, but nothing whatsoever I think I need gloss.

a fiddler's biddin' – a last minute invitation. Here 'at the eleventh hour'.

a perra loonies – a pair of lunatics.

a wee boiling – a small boiled sweet, such as frequently sucked in church.

ablow – below.

Ah'll brekk yir boady – legendary gangfighters threat, goes with Glasgow Kiss.

Ah'll swing for you – I'll volunteer to be hanged for your murder.

Ah'm fair beeling – I'm absolutely boiling with rage.

Ah kennt yir faither – I knew your father, frequently reductive, as in 'do not get above yourself, I know exactly where *you* come from, Jimmy!'.

aye – always – when it doesn't mean yes.

bizzum – a loose, slovenly or bad woman, from a 'besom', a broom, often spelled thus – here a Glasgow phoneticism.

blether – a loquacious talker of nonsense.

bletheranskite – a babbler, a blether, sometimes 'blatherumskite'.

breenge in – barge in.

but – frequently used for 'though'.

clarty-minds – dirty-minds.

clout – hit, clatter round the head.

clype – to tell tales, especially in schools. Also *a clype*, a tell-tale-tit.

come up one's humph – casually occur to one.

coos – cows.

dampt haivering bellum – damned havering beldame. A nag.

daunering – wandering.

daurk – dark.

dinnae fash yirsel – do not worry.

douce – decent, nice, 'perjink'.

dozent – benumbed, stupid.

een – eyes.

ettle – try.

fankle – tangle.

feart – frightened.

fechtin – fighting.

fikey – finicky.

fower – four.

gaberlunzie – a wandering beggarman.

galaday – an outdoor Saturday celebration in a mining village.

gallus – cocky, strutting, flashy – in Glasgow frequently a compliment, esp. of braw new clothes.

galoot – a foolish tall person. Maybe a sarcastic corruption of 'gallant'? Not in the Scots dictionary, but often heard in scornful usage.

gaun like the clappers – going very, very fast indeed .

get a jildy oan – get a move on, hurry up.

gey – very, very.

gey thrawn craturs – very stubborn and contrary creatures.

giein me gyp – causing me a lot of pain (a long-sufferer's complaint as frequently seen in 'Letters to *The Sunday Post* Doctor').

gigot o mutton – a leg of mutton. (Auld Alliance again, French word).

glamourie – fascination.

glisterin – glistening.

gowd and gear – gold and accoutrements. Possessions.

gowpin' – throbbing.

grunzie – face, a (usually unfortunate) visage.

guddle – a muddle, a mess.

guidly – goodly.

guidwife – wife.

hale jingbang – whole kit-and-caboodle.

hansell – a lucky present, or to bless, as in the essential 'hanselling' of a new purse, if given as a present, with a wee coin in it from the donor, for luck.

haud ma jaiket – legendary cry of man about to wade into a fight.

houghmagandie – sexual intercourse. Also 'rumplefyke'. Both suggestive of rough wooing or at very best a jolly tumble lacking in much finesse.

hum and haw – dither and swither. Find it hard to come to a definite decision.

huntigowk – An April Fool Joke. Literally hunt-the-cuckoo.

ilka – each, every.

jackanory – a tall tale, hence a whopper of a lie. Glaswegian kids' slang (from the TV programme, hence here quite unashamedly anachronistic).

jalouse – infer, surmise.

ken – know.

kid-oan – a pretence.

kirk – church.

leein' – lying.

lickerish – liquorice.

lowps – leaps.

lukkin' – looking.

mense – respect, decency.

merrit – married.

my ain twa een – my own two eyes.

onywey – anyway.

Paddy's Market – poor streetmarket in the Irish East End of Glasgow. Hence, colloquially, a disorder.

pair sowell – poor soul.

pyat – a magpie. To see a single one is bad luck of course.

rammy – a riot.

redd it up – tidy it up.

rift – belch, burp.

schunner – an odious, sickening person.

skedaddle – scram.

skelf – a splinter, a sliver. Here a very skinny person.

skinnymalinky – painfully, comically, thin, Skinnymalinky Longlegs being the possessor of the legendary Big Banana Feet.

slaister – a dirty disgusting sloppy mess. Also a 'skiddle'.

slaiverin pee-hereness – lickspittle, slavering, fawning servility.

smeddum – courage, spunk.

smouty – small, insignificant, smout-like.

sook in wi' – suck up to.

sowell – soul.

staunin hoat for houghmagandie – geared up for immediate sexual congress.

stramash – a riot, a rammy.

sumph – a simpleton.

swick – trick, swindle.

thegether – together.

thole – put up with, suffer, stoically endure.

turtledoos – turtle-doves.

tyke – a dog, colloquially a naughty fellow.

umbrelly – umbrella or, as frquently pronounced in West of Scotland, umbarella.

unfashed – untroubled, unworried.

vernear – very nearly; a Lanarkshire/ Glaswegianism.

we never died o winter yet – platitude of foolhardy complacency.

weer the breeks – wear the trousers, be the dominant partner.

whidjies – thingies, whidjamacallits, what-do-you-macallits.

winchin' – courting, wenching.

wyce – right-headed. Usually as in 'you're no wyce'.

yokit – yoked.